CROSSCURRENTS *Modern Critiques*

CROSSCURRENTS *Modern Critiques*
Harry T. Moore, *General Editor*

*William Van O'Connor*

# The New University Wits

## AND THE END OF MODERNISM

**WITH A PREFACE BY**
*Harry T. Moore*

Carbondale

**SOUTHERN ILLINOIS UNIVERSITY PRESS**

## ACKNOWLEDGMENTS

"Aiming at a Million" and "A Note on Wyatt" by Kingsley
Amis are from *A Case of Samples*, copyright © 1956 by
Kingsley Amis. Reprinted by permission of Curtis Brown
Ltd., Victor Gollancz Ltd., and Harcourt, Brace & World,
Inc.

"Gentleman Aged Five before the Mirror" and "When It
Comes" by John Wain are from *A Word Carved on a Sill*,
copyright © 1956 by John Wain. Reprinted by permission
of Routledge & Kegan Paul Ltd.

"Going," "Next, Please," and "Born Yesterday" by Philip
Larkin are from *The Less Deceived*, copyright © 1955 by
The Marvel Press. Reprinted by permission of The Marvel
Press.

"Kings" by Elizabeth Jennings is from *A Way of Looking*,
copyright © 1955 by Elizabeth Jennings. Reprinted by permission of Holt, Rinehart and Winston, Inc., and David
Higham Associates Ltd.

"A Mirror for Poets" by Thom Gunn is from *Fighting Terms*,
copyright © 1957 by Thom Gunn. Reprinted by permission of Faber and Faber Ltd.

"The Evangelist" by Donald Davie is from *New and Selected
Poems*, copyright © 1955 by Donald Davie. Reprinted by
permission of Wesleyan University Press.

"The Landing in Deucalion" by Robert Conquest is from
*Poems*, copyright © 1952 by Robert Conquest. Reprinted
by permission of Macmillan & Co. Ltd. and St. Martin's
Press, Inc.

WILLIAM VAN O'CONNOR, who in recent years has been primarily a commentator on American literature, emerges in the present book as an authoritative historian and critical analyst of the predominant English literary movement since World War II. As Mr. O'Connor demonstrates at the beginning of his study, the participants in this movement should not be called the Angry Young Men, but rather—as Bonamy Dobrée, Walter Allen, and other English critics have suggested—the New University Wits. This doesn't mean that they are preëminently witty, in the usual sense of that word, though at times some of them are, within the range of the common meaning, witty indeed. The title, University Wits, of course refers back to the Oxford and Cambridge men, including Marlowe and Nashe, who became prominent in London literary and theatrical circles during the reign of the earlier Elizabeth.

But what a difference between the two Englands, the one swelling into power and the other shrinking from the status of an empire to that of a small country. Historically, what has happened to England in our time is abnormal. When mighty nations lose their power, historians usually look for reasons within; and these investigators often come up with such findings as failure of nerve. But nothing of this kind happened to England, which was at the height of its moral power when world wars and other conditions of the present age brought about fantastic transformations. Geopolitics can partly explain what happened; inventions that have diminished distances have also contributed. England remains a morally strong, vital country, but in spite of its Commonwealth connections (a kind of private League of Nations which exerts a strong influence in the United Nations), the truth must be faced that England is becoming a small country, as so many of these younger writers want it to be.

They and people like them had nothing to do, of course, with the shrinkage; that, as I pointed out earlier, is attributable to vast and inevitable historical forces which no longer make it possible for a tiny island—John of Gaunt's impregnable fortress in the sea—to dominate a collection of far-flung colonies and, in effect, the world itself. But if these new writers and their families and other families like theirs, working-class groups, are not "responsible" for the diminution of England, they are a symptom of it; and their articulate members, their writers, express new attitudes that define the change.

Some of these attitudes are undeniably angry. A breakdown of the class system occurred in England simultaneously with the breakdown of the empire: there were immediate economic reductions which became social reductions also. This kind of breakdown always brings anger with it for, in times of social upheaval, the formerly suppressed people use their newfound freedom to vent the antagonism that has been so long pent up in them and their forebears. In England this resentment was not murderous because conditions there were not of the hideous kind that inspire murder; England has always essentially had more freedom than most other nations could even imagine. The Magna Carta of 1215 may not have brought about overwhelming reforms, but the document itself was significant, symbolic, and inspiring; and when, in 1649, Cromwell had the head of Charles I chopped off, he ended forever the power of English kings, though the event needed the abdication of James II in 1688 to set a seal on the doom of kingship. Since then, through various generations, the royal family has been largely a show-window family, widely admired and beloved. But in spite of the reduction of the monarchy, the majority of the people still had grievances, for the landowners and the bankers set up an oligarchy which kept the lower classes very much the lower classes. The majority of the people accepted their lot, which was so much better than that of most of their neighbors over on the Continent, though there were a few protests, such as those of the Chartists in the early nineteenth century. But English statesmen, whether Whig, Tory, or Liberal, were usually enlightened, and fought to reduce social and economic evils. And while Continental history of the time is full of uprisings—the years 1830 and 1848 saw monarchs and statesmen fall—there was no serious trouble in England. George Macaulay Trevelyan says there was none because of the Reform Bill of 1832, which "saved the land from revolution and civil strife"; and of course there were later reform bills and similar measures. Yet the class barriers remained.

The foregoing, an example of what the English call potted history, is not a digression but rather a discussion of the background of the New University Wits. For, as Mr. O'Connor shows, most of them came up from the working classes, and many of them are the products of war and the Welfare State. And although some of them went to Oxford and Cambridge, they then went on to teach at the redbrick universities built in the manufacturing cities that had sprung up in the Industrial Revolution. Carl Bode has aptly called these writers "the redbrick Cinderellas."

As Mr. O'Connor shows, not all of them stayed amid the red bricks: John Wain gave up teaching, and so did Kingsley Amis, the latter settling down to write in Oxford, which he had attended as a scholarship man. But I will leave discussion of these matters to Mr. O'Connor, who has given us a rather complete account of the New University Wits themselves, as well as of their writings. I have merely sketched in some historical material.

When we extend these considerations to the twentieth century, we find such writers as Wells, Bennett, and Lawrence among the immediate ancestors of the new group. Of these forerunners, Bennett alone did not come out of poverty; his father, after some vicissitudes in trade, became a solicitor and could afford to send his son to school (as John Wain's father, a well-to-do dentist, could send his son to Oxford). But Wells and Lawrence were scholarship boys, Wells the son of an improvident cricket player and a household servant, Lawrence the son of a coalminer and a former schoolteacher. If Bennett didn't know directly the grinding poverty of the working classes, he knew it from close youthful observation in the pottery towns; but Wells and Lawrence really knew at firsthand what it was to be poor. Bennett became essentially a recorder rather than a man of social protest; Wells became a Fabian and meliorist, though not too violent a one. Like Bennett, he was a best seller and lived well; but he did believe in reform. Lawrence, on the other hand, his natural blitheness often reduced to bitterness by his perpetual ill health, became a vigorous protestant against industrial civilization, and even though he often admired aristocrats and yearned for a new aristocracy of the spirit, he could also inveigh against the upper classes, and some of his bitterest satiric poems attack even accents—the kind now known as "U." Of course Lawrence's attitude was determined by that childhood of privation amid the grime of the collieries. Unlike Bennett or Wells or, for that matter, any of the authors who figure in the present book, Lawrence became a great writer, which sets him apart.

Kingsley Amis may not like him, as Mr. O'Connor shows, but neither Amis nor any of these other young men can get away from the shadow of Lawrence. Most of them grew up, like him, in the Midlands or in the adjacent northern counties (the one young woman Mr. O'Connor treats at length, Iris Murdoch, was born in Dublin; her family had enough money to send her to school, including Somerville College, Oxford). And most of these writers have somewhat the same bias as Lawrence. One feels this very strongly in an author Mr. O'Connor deals with only briefly, one who is not a university man at all—Alan Sillitoe. His finest stories are set in the Nottingham about which Lawrence wrote, and it is interesting to consider the similarities of these two writers as well as their marked differences; the hero of Sillitoe's Saturday Night and Sunday Morning is a less sensitive descendant of the hero of Sons and Lovers. Of course Lawrence's poetic intensity carries him beyond the range of Sillitoe, but the central figure in each of the novels referred to has many of the same problems. In Sillitoe they are less psychological and more social. In Sons and Lovers, Paul Morel's protest, such as it is, represents an effort to free the individual from psychological shackles; he merely exists amid social conditions which also hamper the individual. On the other hand, Arthur Seaton, in

Saturday Night and Sunday Morning, exists almost entirely within the confines of the sociological. Lawrence's book is a Künstlerroman, a novel about an artist, hardly a representative individual; Sillitoe's book deals with a more typical victim of repressive social conditions. Both young men work in Nottingham factories, yet Arthur, in spite of those social restrictions, has greater freedom than Paul, among other reasons because he makes comparatively more money under the new dispensation. Yet he is always in a rage against conditions: "There's bound to be trouble in store for me every day of my life, because trouble it's always been and always will be." Paul is nearly crushed by his psychological problems, yet at the end he turns away from the temptation of death and walks back "towards the faintly humming, glowing town, quickly" —quickly in Lawrence's usage being an observance of the Biblical employment of the word, suggesting that Paul was resolutely returning to life. Arthur Seaton, despite his bitterness, finds that "it's a good life and a good world, all said and done, if you don't weaken" —a somewhat Darwinian concept of the kind not ordinarily found in Lawrence.

It was not until after Sons and Lovers that Lawrence actively directed his hatred against the dominance of industrialism and of the Establishment (a word he did not use). Ironically, too many of the younger people of England today, taking their attitudes from Lawrence, miss the eloquence and poetry with which he expressed his own—the poetry which is intrinsic to the best of Lawrence. I can remember, a few years ago, leaving Venice by train and meeting, in the railway carriage, a young English married couple who had been on a tour; they were schoolteachers and avid socialists; and, as we talked while the train rattled across Lombardy, I discovered they were admirers of

Lawrence. But they were not acquainted with his great novels, The Rainbow and Women in Love, or his charming travel volumes, or, indeed, very much of his work at all. The one book they did know was Pansies, the unpoetic but often vital little verses Lawrence wrote toward the end of his life. I tried to explain that, whatever the virtues of the Pansies poems, they were secondary or even tertiary Lawrence; but the young socialist couple were unimpressed. They happily quoted "How Beastly the Bourgeois Is" and other verses from Pansies, and to them this was Lawrence, as it probably is to many of the newer school of English writers.

These writers do seem unaware of the force of language, as they seem unaware of what the larger vision is; the kind of vision, that is, which Lawrence possessed. The New University Wits, except Iris Murdoch at times, seem scarcely interested in writing as writing, or in the bigger questions, in which attitude they resemble most American authors now living, though not the somewhat older British writers such as Elizabeth Bowen, Graham Greene, and Lawrence Durrell. The New University Wits have their little stories to tell, stories which are pertinent and interesting, but almost always provincial or parochial; and for the most part they tell these stories flatly, in a colloquial manner that requires none of the effort of more intensified writing and that in its very littleness precludes the entrance of the larger vision.

But these writers do constitute an interesting chapter in the history of English literature, as Mr. O'Connor ably demonstrates. He writes of his subject with interest and eagerness, but he never abandons his critical obligations, and so gives us not only history but continual evaluation, as when he so rightly says that John Wain's novels read like an effort of the will, or when he plays down Kingsley Amis's poetry and points out that Amis's first and fourth novels are far better than his second and third—and so on. But now it is time to let Mr. O'Connor treat these matters in detail, with the valuable thoroughness and judiciousness that characterize his work.

However limited the achievements of these New University Wits may be, the group offers material for an absorbing study; these writers reflect an important part of their time; among other things they represent, in the Ortega sense, a revolt of the masses. Mr. O'Connor gives us the particulars of all this, and does so with consistently helpful insights, for William Van O'Connor expertly combines the rôles of historian and critic. It is rare to have a book on a current subject that probes it so skillfully, and with results so rewarding.

HARRY T. MOORE

University of Colorado
November 22, 1962

# CONTENTS

|    | PREFACE | *v* |
|----|---------|-----|
|    | INTRODUCTION | *xv* |
| 1  | A NEW LITERARY GENERATION | 3 |
| 2  | PHILIP LARKIN: The Quiet Poem | 16 |
| 3  | JOHN WAIN: The Will to Write | 30 |
| 4  | IRIS MURDOCH: The Formal and the Contingent | 54 |
| 5  | KINGSLEY AMIS: That Uncertain Feeling | 75 |
| 6  | THE OTHER WRITERS: A Common View | 103 |
| 7  | THE NEW HERO AND A SHIFT IN LITERARY CONVENTIONS | 133 |
| 8  | A POSTSCRIPT: Period Styles | 150 |
|    | NOTES | 159 |
|    | INDEX | 165 |

THE SITUATION of writers in England after World War II has been distinctly different from what it was after World War I. The particular writers with whom we are concerned in this book, sometimes called the Movement and sometimes called the New University Wits, have experienced the social and cultural shifts of the Welfare State, and their writings reflect and interpret these changes.

Almost all of them have or have had university connections. The majority have been scholarship students. Most of them come from working-class or lower middle-class families. They matured during and after World War II, and they have lived in the Welfare State. They are a part of a different, a broadened, more democratized, culture than England has had in the past.

A book similar in many ways to this one could have been written about such writers as Angus Wilson, Charles Snow, and others. They too show us a newer England and exhibit changed literary conventions. Some of the advantages in writing about The New University Wits is that they form a group, generally represent a new class in English literary life, and came of age after World War II. Naturally they do not speak for their entire generation in England. No group does. Yet anyone interested in the history of English literature can see that they, the question of their abilities aside, are as clearly the voices of the 1950's in England as Eliot and Pound were for the 1920's, Auden and Spender for the 1930's, and Dylan Thomas for the 1940's. Several members of the group have already done notable work, and, considering their talents, it seems likely they will go on to do more and possibly even better work. Something can be said for the achievements of all of them. What is perfectly clear is that their assumptions and their conventions are very different from the assumptions and conventions of their eminent elders, Yeats, Eliot, Lawrence or Virginia Woolf. They tended to dominate the 1950's in English letters, and as a group exhibit the ways in which poetry, fiction and criticism caught the life of those ten years.

There are a number of books by these writers that have appeared recently which I note only in passing. Although it is tempting to treat each new publication as a book goes down to the wire, I believe the temptation, in this case, should be resisted. The focus of the study is on the 1950's, and attempting to incorporate the beginnings of the 1960's would invite a different focus, and finally a different book from this one.

William Van O'Connor

University of California
Davis

The New University Wits, and the End of Modernism

# 1   A NEW LITERARY
       GENERATION

THE POPULAR PRESS and a good many literary publications in England have called the creators of the new hero the Angry Young Men. According to John Wain, "Angry Young Man" was "originally applied to Mr. Woodrow Wyatt, a politician, and subsequently extended far enough to include on the one hand a handful of poets, dramatists and novelists, and on the other such figures as Mr. Colin Wilson and the late James Dean." Obviously this category, if it is one, is pretty loose. Wain says the coinage, and the copy it made possible, was a journalistic stunt.

A great deal has also been made of a group called the "Movement." This term is usually taken to mean, one, the novels written by Philip Larkin, Kingsley Amis, John Wain, and Iris Murdoch, two, the poets who appeared in *Poets of the 1950's* (1955), edited by Dennis Enright, and *New Lines* (1956), edited by Robert Conquest, and three, the criticism and manifestos written by these poets and novelists. Most of them either are or have been university lecturers (two are university librarians)—and as a consequence have also been called the "New University Wits." In an article published in 1954 on contemporary English poetry, Bonamy Dobrée said that Donald Davie, John Wain, Kingsley Amis and Dennis Enright, all academics, had been called the New University Wits. Walter Allen, in a British Council pamphlet, *The Novel Today*, treats Wain, Amis and Iris Murdoch under the heading "University Wits." University Wits seems the preferable term, since it does not carry the connotation, as Movement does, of "bandwagon" or "mutual admiration society." But Movement is the term that has been more widely used.

Stephen Spender, in the November 1953, issue of *Encounter*, wrote a short piece entitled "On Literary Movements." England, he said, was experiencing "a rebellion of the Lower Middle Brows." It was, he said, a revolt against London literary life, against traditional intellectual trends at Oxford and Cambridge, against the poets of the 1930's and the 1940's, and against the cosmopolitan spirit in modern literature. Essentially, he said, it was a revolt against the "classy." Ironically, the supporters of the revolution were mostly redbrick or provincial university lecturers. Spender said that the snobbishness of the literary world had been responsible for "this new provincial puritanism as the Regency Rakes were for the respectable Victorians." But not for a moment could he entertain the notion that the new movement might be desirable. The reason for this had nothing to do with their tenets or point of view—it was that they were teachers. "There is one good reason for doubting whether university teachers will bring life to literature: they might confuse literature with lecturing about literature."

Spender did not mention any writers by name— and it remained for *The Spectator* to identify some of those who were to be labelled Movement writers. Anthony Hartley, in concluding a general article in *The Spectator* entitled "Poets of the Fifties," [1] said, "we are now in the presence of the only considerable

movement in English poetry since the 'Thirties'."
Among others, he had discussed John Wain, Donald
Davie, Thom Gunn, and Philip Larkin. He observed
their "complication of thought, austerity of tone,
colloquialism, and avoidance of rhetoric." In the
background, he said, were Empson and Leavis.

Several weeks later, an anonymous article, also in
*The Spectator*,[2] upper-cased "movement." It was en-
titled "In the Movement." From this point on, the
Movement has existed, as fact or fiction or a mixture
of the two. The article identified Movement writers
not merely as poets but as the creators of the "new
Hero who is basically irresponsible." The question of
responsibility aside, at this point five Movement nov-
els had appeared: Larkin's *Jill* and *A Girl in Winter*,
Wain's *Hurry On Down*, Amis' *Lucky Jim*, and Miss
Iris Murdoch's *Under the Net*. The article quoted
Walter Allen on the origin of the new hero: "The
Services, certainly, helped to make him; but George
Orwell, Dr. Leavis and the Logical Positivists—or,
rather, the attitudes these represented—all contributed to his genesis." According to the article, the
Movement was still incohesive "and, as a movement,
dumb"—but it existed. Its poets and novelists were
opposed to the political preoccupations of the Thirties, and to the lush writing of the Forties. They
poked fun, with an off-handed toughness, at almost
everyone and everything. "But the Movement is interesting. It is interesting, like other movements, not
only in itself, but because of the light which it throws
upon the work of writers who are outside of it, perhaps opposed to it. And small as it is, it is nevertheless
a part of the movement of that tide which is pulling
us through the Fifties and toward the Sixties."

Two weeks later, the Letters to the Editor pages
were filled with comments on "In the Movement."

One of Mr. Davie's colleagues at the University College, Dublin, pointed out that these poets were not merely reacting against the poetry of the Thirties and Forties, they were deliberately emulating the virtues of late eighteenth-century poetry. And he added: to understand the Movement, it is necessary "to describe, with detailed examples, the various attitudes, tones and assumptions exemplified in the works of such writers as Mr. Davie, Mr. Gunn, Mr. Wain, Miss Murdoch, and Mr. Amis."

G. S. Fraser noted that the new hero was irascible, and that his anger was "directed fundamentally against the difficulty of leading a good life in modern society." He added that a wide range of styles are observable among the poets (only two or three being Empsonian). But to the outsider, they "do seem to have in common a cagey and cautious attitude, an ironical defensiveness, directed toward the possible reader and their own inner feelings."

Malcolm Bradbury, in a Spectator article, made the point that these writers were for the most part "academic writer-critics" and as such needed a magazine similar to one of the American quarterlies. The London journals, he added, especially Mr. Spender's *Encounter*, had gone out of their way to be hostile to these new writers. Asked to identify the author or authors of the anonymous "In the Movement," Ian Gilmour, the editor, replied: "The chief author of the article in question was J. D. Scott, but I. Hamilton and others in the office had a hand in it." And he added: "Indeed I think *The Spectator* 'invented' the movement."

Certain of the Movement writers also believe it was "invented." Philip Larkin has said, "We are all perfectly convinced that the name at any rate took its origin in a piece of sheer journalism in *The Spectator*."

And Thom Gunn, writing of his relations with the various Movement poets, has said, "I was certainly not aware that I was supposed to be associated with the Movement until 1954, when I first saw the word used of us." Wain says that if there is a movement he can understand grouping Amis, Larkin and himself—but he can't see why Iris Murdoch should be lumped with them. Donald Davie has said he believes the first suggestion of a group came with John Wain's "First Reading," a program on the B.B.C. in 1953, and that the seal was put on the movement with the Enright and Conquest anthologies.

Some of the listeners to "First Reading" accused Wain of pushing his friends, or at least pushing writers who held critical positions similar to his own. In two of his weekly columns in the *New Statesman and Nation*, Hugh Massingham said Wain was attempting a literary *coup*:

> Our brave new world is over at last and the old fogies can be led off to the slaughter-house after being festooned with the usual sacrificial garlands. After that Mr. Wain and his fledglings can move in and establish the new dispensation. . . .
> Is there not something faintly ridiculous in treating young men, whom some of us never have heard of, with the solemnity that should be reserved for Mr. Eliot and Mr. Empson?

Mr. Massingham also said that Mr. Wain and his contributors (those who read their poems, fiction and criticism on his program) were extremely provincial.

Several among those who wrote letters about Massingham's articles made the point that Wain's young writers were mostly "young dons." This led to letters about the proper meaning of "don." And this, in turn, led to discussions of the "sociological perspective" of these writers. Wain himself stated their "perspective"

quite vividly: "It is true that a few of my contributors
are employed by provincial universities. But a provincial university lecturer is not a 'don.' . . . I myself sit,
as I compile 'First Reading,' not in a gracious panelled
room overlooking a beautiful quadrangle, but in a tiny
slum-clearance bungalow. It happens to be where I
live."

John Lehmann, who had had a similar program on
the B.B.C., and has been a professional discoverer of
new talents, had his say. In the opening sentence of his
letter he says he hesitated to "enter the lists" in the
controversy, but before finishing he finds Mr. Wain's
contributors "third-rate." G. S. Fraser was more generous, explaining that this was the newest generation
of writers, young men who "hoped to storm London
with their pens." Wain stuck to his guns, defending
his contributors: "My contributors are not chosen *because* they are young and unknown—it just happens to
be a peculiarity of our period that the tendencies offering the best hope for English literature are to be
seen most clearly in the work of younger men."

Several years later, in December, 1956, Wain had
another word to say about his part in the Third Programme. The occasion was his review of *From the
Third Programme, A Ten-Years' Anthology*,[3] edited
by John Morris. Wain disapproves of the dilettantism
of Mr. Morris and deplores his failure to include some
of the serious criticism and serious poetry that had
been read on the Third Programme. Then he gets into
the matter of the program he had edited:

> The present literary generation is the first one in the
> history of English literature, and quite possibly the last,
> to have made its *debut* by means of broadcasting. When
> I say 'present generation,' of course I know that there
> are always two or three generations on the scene at
> once, and I mean the fairly young ones, those who are

now in their thirties. Some representative names would be: A. Alvarez, Kingsley Amis, Anthony Hartley, Philip Larkin, Mairi MacInnes, Philip Oakes, Burns Singer. Every one of these writers, all of whom are squarely before the public eye to-day, was introduced to a wider public on the Third Programme; it doesn't behoove me to talk about it, because I edited the series, called *First Reading,* in which they all appeared; in any case all that happened, as far as I was concerned, was that I was savaged from all sides. . . . However, it is a fact that the very people who are now dominant were unknown before they became the centre of controversy in these six programmes. . . . This is an interesting point of intersection between the history of broadcasting and the history of literature.

The first of the two Movement anthologies was Enright's *Poets of the 1950's.*[4] Enright says that in editing the volume he had no sense of being part of a movement: "I don't think there was a movement back in those days, or if there was, I didn't know about it, as I was in Japan and very rarely saw *The Spectator.*" He says he wanted only to put together an anthology of young poets "who steered between the rock of Wastelanditis and the whirlpool of Dylanitis." Having listed seven poets whose work he found congenial, he wrote to Robert Conquest ("the only English poet I had met in the flesh") asking for advice. Conquest listed a few possibilities but made no strong recommendations. Shortly afterwards, Macmillan commissioned Conquest to edit *New Lines.*[5] He printed the same eight poets, adding only Thom Gunn. The similarity between the two volumes, according to Enright, has been interpreted "as part of a sinister plot to 'take over' English poetry." There was, Enright says, "no collusion." He did not include Thom Gunn because at the time he had not read him. Of the choice of poets he says, "Who else, in that generation, is there to choose?"

Enright's eight poets were Amis, a St. John's College (Oxford) graduate, and then (that is, in 1955) Lecturer in English at University College, Swansea; Robert Conquest, Magdalen College, Oxford, and a member of the Foreign Office; Donald Davie, Cambridge, and Fellow of Trinity College, Dublin; John Holloway, All Souls, Oxford, and Lecturer at Cambridge; Elizabeth Jennings, Oxford, and a librarian at Oxford; Philip Larkin, St. John's, Oxford, and Librarian at Hull; John Wain, St. John's College, Oxford, and Lecturer in English at the University of Reading; and Enright himself, Downing College, Cambridge (he was a student of Leavis'), and Visiting Professor at Konan University in Japan. Thom Gunn was a Cambridge graduate, a student at Stanford, and then a member of the English Department of the University of California at Berkeley.

In 1952, Enright had written some favorable comments on Conquest's poems. The occasion was a review of a P.E.N. volume, *New Poems 1951*. Before Enright left, in 1953, for a three year stay in Japan, they met on two occasions. He had also been impressed by Philip Larkin's *XX Poems* (1951) and had wanted to meet him—"but Larkin's shyness prevented it." Enright returned to England in the summer of 1956. At Oxford he got to know Wain (both were tutoring), Elizabeth Jennings, and, very briefly, Amis. In 1957, after a ten month teaching stint in Berlin, he met Amis again, and also Gunn. He has yet to meet Holloway, Davie, or Larkin. "So much," he says, "for this notion of blood-thirsty blood brothers."

Robert Conquest believes the term Movement, as used in *The Spectator* article, was meant to designate "people like Wain, Alvarez, George McBeth, Bernard

Bergonzi," and to some extent Amis, poets who employed "rich Empsonian ambiguities." (The article, however, does not mention these poets, except for Wain and Amis, nor does it describe Movement poetry as being solely Empsonian.) Conquest believes this original group based itself on Wain's study of Empson, published in *Penguin New Writing* in 1950. He adds:

> These are the people I am talking about in the fifth section of my introduction to New Lines (and, in fact, in the original draft, I spoke of them as poets known as the Movement, thus making explicit what is in any case implicit, that I didn't regard New Lines as in any way 'Movement' in the sense the word was then used. Owing to my final failure to put it down in black and white the term was transferred to the poets I have collected in New Lines.

Conquest does not believe any great harm was done by the new usage, except that it made for some confusion: "Such things as—The Movement by definition writes academic terza rima like Wain; Dennis Enright is a member of the Movement; therefore he writes terza rima (or alternatively why *doesn't* he write terza rima?)" Conquest says he printed Wain "in spite of his Movement-in-the-old-sense methods, not because of them." The poets in *New Lines*, he says, were selected because they have something in common: *New Lines* poets prefer "the language of men" to "howl and cypher," do "not exclude direct statement," and disavow the "disruptive notion that anything can symbolize anything."

When he undertook to edit *New Lines*, Conquest knew personally only Enright, Amis, Wain and Elizabeth Jennings. He had met Amis, then quite unknown, at a party, and shortly came to admire his poetry. He and Wain had met and corresponded, and he had met Elizabeth Jennings while editing some of her poems for a yearly *P.E.N. Anthology* (1953). Quite clearly the poets in the Enright and Conquest anthologies were not, for the most part, a closely knit group of friends. The friendships have grown out of critical views held in common—and undoubtedly out of the accident of their being seen as a Movement and thus sharing a common fate.

The *Times Literary Supplement* reviewed the two anthologies together. The reviewer said neither anthology attempted to be inclusive—they are, he said, "programme anthologies." These poets are "makers rather than bards." Further, he pointed out that by and large they were humanistic not religious, liberal not radical or reactionary, cool not fervid, sceptical not enthusiastic, empirical not transcendental. "It is in many ways admirable, and certainly a traditionally English temper of mind, but what is surprising is to put it forward as a typically poetic one." This is an excellent characterization of the group. There is no mention of Movement.

But other periodicals referred to Movement in reviews, articles, and letters to the editor. A number of readers were irritated by the prefaces or little manifestoes in the Enright volume. Actually, many points of view appear—but common to most of them is self-satisfaction with their craftsmanship and a sense that the immediate future of English poetry is now in the hands of the Movement. Many readers who have come to see modern poetry as involved not merely with French Symbolism but somehow with all of Western culture were disturbed by the forthright provincialism of several of the prefaces.

Naturally too, some poets of the same generation whose work was not represented by Enright or Conquest felt themselves victimized. Dannie Abse and Howard Sargeant edited *Maverick* (1957) as a kind of answer. These editors recommended "a dreadful struggle . . . between the poem and the poet, between the nameless, amorphous, Dionysian material and the conscious, law abiding articulating craftsmen." This is a statement Movement poets would greet with derision.

At this point, we should ask whether the Movement owes its "existence" to *The Spectator* and to reveiwers and literary gossips. All literary movements owe their existence in part to fortuitous events, and certainly all of them exist as legend plus fact. The Movement is no exception. Perhaps there is a comparison to be made between the Movement and the Bloomsbury group.

Reviewers, critics, and literary historians commonly refer to the Bloomsbury group—Virginia Woolf, E. M. Forster, Lytton Strachey, John Maynard Keynes, Desmond MacCarthy, Clive Bell, David Garnett, and others. It is assumed that these writers not only were friendly with each other but held critical tenets in common. Books and articles are written, tracing the King's College, Cambridge, beginnings of Bloomsbury (the Midnight Society), later meetings of the group in London, new friends being introduced, and discussing their doctrines, achievements and collective influence. One may be a little surprised, therefore, in reading essays by MacCarthy, Bell, and Mrs. Woolf, to find them denying that there was any such thing as the Bloomsbury group.

The Bloomsbury writers, with their upper middle-class backgrounds, their dedication to art, and their close personal relationships, have seemed sufficiently a "collectivity" (it is Keynes' term) to justify their being discussed as a group. The Movement writers have seemed sufficiently alike to justify discussion of them as a group. Many serious critics both of the novel and of poetry have borne witness to its existence.

If we are to locate a point in history when the first

inklings of a movement are perceptible it would be at St. John's College, Oxford, during the 1940's. Kingsley Amis and Philip Larkin first knew each other there in 1941. During 1942–45, Amis was in the army, but he visited Oxford occasionally on leaves. They became good friends early and have remained so. Naturally not all of their critical tenets or judgments are alike. But Larkin says they have almost always agreed on what they find funny or derisible. *Lucky Jim* is dedicated to Larkin. And Larkin's *XX Poems* is dedicated to Amis. Wain too was at St. John's, beginning there in 1943. Larkin was to graduate in a few weeks—but he, like Amis, returned for visits and Wain got to know both of them. Amis' *A Frame of Mind* is dedicated to Wain, and Wain's *The Contenders* is dedicated to Larkin. Probably it would be an error to stress their immediate influence on one another as writers. On the other hand, they had the common experience of attending a college, St. John's, that was peopled largely by scholarship students. The students at St. John's were serious, and there was little of what Amis calls the "exclusive spirit" operating. If King's College, at the turn of the century, with its Midnight Society, serves as a little Bloomsbury symbol, then St. John's College, during wartime, can serve as a little symbol of the Movement.

A second point of emergence was Wain's "First Reading" on the B.B.C. in 1953. His contributors had included Amis and Larkin. Critics of the program seem to have been disturbed by the youth of the contributors and by the fact that some of them were university lecturers. No one seems to have labelled the program itself Movement—but Anthony Hartley grouped some of the contributors in his "Poets of the Fifties," in 1954. Obviously the two anthologies had their origins independently of Amis, Larkin, and Wain. One of the interesting things about the collections is that Conquest and Enright arrived independently at similar points of view and sought out not only each other but the St. John's College group.

By the end of the 1950's the members of the group necessarily tended to go their separate ways. English writers, however, have always tended to make a great deal about the way their college and university stamped them, and the way they were influenced by their immediate contemporaries. The New University Wits are no exception.

The Bloomsbury writers pointed out that not all of them had attended King's College, Cambridge—a few had attended Oxford colleges; they also pointed out that not all of them were descended from eminent upper middle-class Victorian families; and they insisted on pointing to what was unique in the work of each writer. Movement writers have pointed out that not all of them are from Oxford—a few are from Cambridge; they also insist that not all of them are from working-class families or even are scholarship students; and they insist on their individual differences. Despite the protests, literary historians and critics have treated Bloomsbury writers as a group—and the chances are that the Movement writers will continue to be treated as a group. As a group, they are preoccupied with social and cultural shifts in Welfare State England, and with their consequences. It does not follow, of course, that this is their sole interest. It is undoubtedly true, as Robert Conquest has said, that "class has blurred a pretty fair amount (though not by any means entirely) in England." This blurring is a part of the new environment with which Movement writers concern themselves. Characteristically, their approach to all problems, social or literary, is hard-headed, realistic, even satiric.

THE 1920's saw the emergence of T. S. Eliot and Ezra Pound, the 1930's Wystan Auden, Louis MacNeice and Stephen Spender, the 1940's Dylan Thomas. Each decade has had a distinctive idiom and distinctive conventions. The 1950's, the post-World War II decade, has had no "big" poets. Upon looking into the matter, one discovers that a number of poets now writing seem to oppose bigness or even the idea of major poets almost as a matter of principle. Sir Herbert Read has said, "The poetry of the 1950's ought not to raise its voice." The poets in *Poets of the 1950's* and *New Lines* do not raise their voices. Perhaps the most characteristic as well as the best of them is Philip Larkin.

Larkin's reputation is probably greater than that of any of his contemporaries. His *The Less Deceived*, published in England in 1955, and here in 1958, has been highly praised. It is not well known, at least in America, that he is the author of two volumes of fiction, *Jill* and *A Girl in Winter*. Apparently he has given up fiction writing in order to address his attention more fully to poetry. However the two novels are worth examining if only because they may shed some light on his practices as a poet. But first a word about his career.

Philip Larkin was born in Coventry, August 9,

1922, and lived there for eighteen years. His father was the City Treasurer. Larkin attended King Henry VIII school for ten years, 1930 to 1940. "I was," he says, "very stupid until I could concentrate on English." In *The Less Deceived,* there is a poem entitled "I Remember, I Remember." It provides a good introduction to Larkin's wry humor. The poem opens—

> *Coming up England by a different line*
> *For once, early in the cold new year,*
> *We stopped, and, watching men with number plates*
> *Sprint down the platform to familiar gates,*
> *'Why, Coventry!' I exclaimed. 'I was born there.'*

The following six stanzas are a joshing treatment of a writer's boyhood as commonly found in biographies. None of the exciting things that might have happened did happen.

> *'You look as if you wished the place in Hell,'*
> *My friend said, 'judging from your face.' 'Oh, well,*
> *I suppose it's not the place's fault,' I said.*

> *'Nothing, like something, happens anywhere.'*

Larkin was rejected by the army, and went up to St. John's, Oxford, in 1940. Not a scholarship student, he nonetheless took a first in English. At St. John's, he and Kingsley Amis were close friends. Larkin says he and Amis also went through a period of "intensive joke swapping just after the war." He was also friendly with John Wain.

Larkin's first job, lasting three years, was as a librarian in a small Shropshire town, Wellington. There he got into the habit of writing from nine to midnight. *The North Ship* (1945) [1] was his first book. Of it, he says, "It was equally compounded of W. B. Yeats and of having nothing to say." *Jill,*[2] a short novel about

Oxford, appeared in 1946, and A *Girl in Winter*,[3] the following year. Larkin intended to continue writing fiction, but discovered that he preferred to give his attention to poetry. He finishes only four or five poems a year, but the acclaim he has received, especially for *The Less Deceived*,[4] indicates that his decision may have been right.

Larkin has held other posts. From 1946 to 1950 he was assistant librarian at the University College of Leicester. His next post was at Queen's University, Belfast. While at Belfast, he produced a privately printed collection of poems, *XX Poems* (1951). Copies were sent to many well-known literary figures, but none of them took notice of it publicly. A pamphlet, *Fantasy: 21*,[5] was published in 1954. In 1955, Larkin was appointed librarian at the University of Hull. Larkin says that having a regular profession has probably helped discipline him, thus enabling him to write regularly. He has no ambition to teach, and in fact will go to almost any length to avoid giving a public talk.

## ii

*Jill* is the story of a small town boy (from Huddlesford), John Kemp, who goes to Oxford, at Michaelmas Term 1940, on a scholarship. He is extremely shy and sensitive. At Huddlesford Grammar School, he has been singled out by Mr. Crouch, a Cambridge man, as a bright, promising student. Crouch had heard the mathematics master describe Kemp thus: "Why, yes. A very good all-round intelligence, there. Picks up knowledge like a magnet picks up iron filings. His father's a policeman, I think—or was. I know they aren't well off." Kemp had worked tirelessly—and when the war started he was able to take and win an Open Scholarship exam a year ahead of schedule.

Kemp is not up to adjusting to University life. He is terribly intimidated by his roommate, Christopher Warner, a thick-skinned, vicious lout. The story is concerned with his shyness and the consequences of it. Warner has been to a preparatory school, but one that was not, according to another scholarship student, Whitbread, very high in the social scale. Kemp finds Whitbread almost as disconcerting as he finds Warner and Warner's cronies. Whitbread is both very bright and "on the make." He gives Kemp all sorts of advice. "John was impressed, but also slightly embarrassed: Whitbread's eagerness was embarrassing: it was like watching a man scouring his plate with a piece of bread." Crouch, during a visit to Oxford, also turns out to be something of an opportunist—he gives Kemp advice about how to make "contacts" that will be helpful after his University days. The War does not intrude very obviously into the Oxford term—except for Kemp's return to Huddlesford when he learns it has been badly bombed. His family has not been injured, and he returns to Oxford the same day.

The story line is rather slight—and as Larkin himself says, "despite its length," the book "remains in essence an unambitious short story." John Kemp is a fish out of water. Unlike Whitbread, he has no knack for "getting on." The effrontery and bad manners of Warner and his crowd cause him to turn in on himself and to live a strange fantasy life. The chief element in this is the creation of a sister, Jill: he writes a diary of the sort she might have kept, writes her letters (to impress Warner), writes a short story about her school life—and finally he "sees" her in an Oxford street.

The girl he actually sees is a fifteen year old named Gillian, a cousin to Elizabeth, whom Warner is trying to seduce. Gillian remains Jill so far as Kemp is concerned. He is frustrated in his desire to see much of her. After a drinking bout, he seeks her out at a party and kisses her. Warner and his friends throw him into a fountain. As a consequence of the dousing, he becomes ill, although not seriously, and is hospitalized. The term is ending, and the final scenes present his parents seeking him out and Christopher Warner, with Elizabeth in tow, heading for London. There is the implication, in Kemp's feverish dreams, that he will never quite manage to control "the maddened surface of things."

A number of the scenes in *Jill* are well done, and several of the characterizations are excellent. The University life, on its various levels, is evoked with skill. But Kemp's fantasy about Jill is not very convincing. The reader feels acutely Kemp's shyness but there is insufficient preparation for his sudden retreat into fantasy. Despite Larkin's skill, which is considerable, the action remains incredible.

*A Girl in Winter* is a much better novel. It creates and sustains a mood of almost unalleviated dreariness and frustration. England, one Saturday in wartime, is covered with snow. Outside there is frost and intense cold. Inside, there is dirt, dinginess, and quiet despair.

Katherine Lind, foreign-born and trained, is working in a small public library. Mr. Anstey, the acting director, is an ugly-tempered petty tyrant, and as the novel opens he is berating Miss Lind about a book that has been misplaced. Only later does one learn that he has a streak of generosity. Even this hardly modifies the impression one has of him as a mean-spirited man filled with a sense of inadequacy and driven by it. They are interrupted by the news that one of the young employees, Miss Green, is ill with a severe tooth-ache. Anstey allows Katherine to accompany Miss Green, either to the girl's home or to a dentist.

Katherine is glad to escape. They find a dentist who is as unpleasant as Anstey, and whose office, if possible, is more dreary than the library. The removal of Miss Green's tooth is described in awesome detail. And the glimpses Katherine gets into Miss Green's life show it to be not entirely cheerless, yet mean and straitened.

The one promise of pleasure in Katherine's life is the possibility of renewing a friendship with the Fennels, a family she had visited, coming from her home on the continent six years earlier. She and Robin Fennel had exchanged letters as a kind of school exercise, and the visit had followed. After her return home she and the Fennels had lost track of each other and upon coming back to England as an adult she had not tried to re-establish the relationship. Then, on impulse, she had written. Mrs. Fennel and Jane, Robin's sister, had replied, sending their best wishes, and they had sent Robin's army address. On the morning of her excursion with Miss Green, Katherine is expecting a letter from him.

Back in her room, which is over a chemist's shop, Katherine finds the letter and learns that Robin plans to arrive later that day. Book two follows. It is a flashback account of her visit with the Fennels when she was sixteen. There is a fine evocation of a young girl visiting in a foreign country. She and Robin visit Oxford (the Fennels live in Oxfordshire), go to a horse-show, punt on the river that flows through the Fennel property, have a puppy-love affair, and Jane becomes engaged to a stuffy young man, Jack Stormalong.

Book three is prefaced, as is book one, by a description of the snow:

It was not romantic or picturesque: the snow that was graceful in the country, was days old in the town: it had been trodden to a brown powder and shovelled into gutters. Where it had not been disturbed, on burnt out buildings, on warehouse roofs or sheds in the warehouse yards, it made the scene more dingy and dispirited.

The Katherine who awaits Robin feels empty and surrounded by meaninglessness.

During the morning expedition in search of a dentist, Miss Green had accidentally exchanged purses with a Miss Veronica Parbury. Katherine undertakes to return the purse and to get Miss Green's. A letter in Miss Parbury's purse appears to have been written by Mr. Anstey. Miss Parbury ("she looked like a large tea-rose gone well to seed") cares for her invalid mother. She refuses to put the mother in a home, or to allow Mr. Anstey to take on the responsibility for her mother. Katherine, who learns about this largely by inferences, quarrels with Miss Parbury because she sees the sacrifice as a sort of self-persecution. When she returns to the library she learns that Miss Green has already returned to work, and Katherine's lateness gives Anstey another opportunity to reprimand her. She replies angrily and purposely insults him by saying he should save his fatuous advice for his "silly Veronica Parbury." The rest of the afternoon goes slowly and painfully—until the lights are put out at seven o'clock and the staff leaves.

At her room, she finds Robin. He has had to wait a long time and has been drinking in a nearby pub. The Robin she had known during her visit had been proper and rather pompous—now he is given to self-pity. They are not able to recover their earlier sense of friendship. Robin tries to make love to her but she repulses him. She learns that Jane has lost a child under especially painful circumstances, and her marriage has not gone very well. But in their own misery Katherine and Robin soon forget about Jane. When he asks to spend the night, she is neither flattered nor insulted. She allows it under the condition that he is not to try to make love to her. In bed, they talk about the frustrations the war has caused. Then they fall off to sleep. In the closing paragraphs, their dreams and hopes are shown mixing somehow with the snow and finally resting on iceflows in a lightless channel.

Larkin relies neither on violence nor the bizarre. Nothing outwardly momentous happens, but the frustrations of a half-dozen or more characters emerge clearly, if not exactly poignantly. Occasionally there is a touch of compassion, but there is no effort to see the characters either warmly or sentimentally. Katherine's summer visit had had its problems but in retrospect it seems almost bright and happy. On page after page, there is unrelieved drabness. No single character sees a way out of his impasse.

The theme of *A Girl in Winter* is expressed in the statement that ultimately a sense of peace is to be found in facing one's frustrations: "Unsatisfied dreams rose and fell about them, crying out against their implacability, but in the end glad that such order, such destiny existed. Against this knowledge, the heart, the will, and all that made for protest, could at last sleep." *A Girl in Winter* is not merely an image of a country in wartime; it is an image of human beings making peace with all that is inexorable and implacable, making peace with their lives and their deaths. Larkin's view of human destiny, in the novel at least, includes very little that is joyous or high-spirited. *A Girl in Winter*, a beautifully written story, is disturbing, and, in many respects, undoubtedly true. But a reader can feel justified in complaining that the theme—that people do make terms with their defeats—is not large enough as Larkin treats it. He seems to have intended to show that defeat is finally accompanied, or can be, by a glimmer of joy, but he did not manage to get this glimmer into his novel.

### iii

Larkin's development as a poet has not been untypical. *The North Ship* is a mixture of Housman, Hardy, and Yeats. This is a sample:

> To wake, and hear a cock
> Out of the distance crying,
> To pull the curtains back
> And see the clouds flying—
> How strange it is
> For the heart to be loveless, and as cold as these.

*The North Ship* is filled with romantic décor of this sort.

A characteristic later poem is "Going":

> There is an evening coming in
> Across the fields, one never seen before,
> That lights no lamps.
>
> Silken it seems at a distance, yet
> When it is drawn up over the knees and breast
> It brings no comfort.
>
> Where has the tree gone, that locked
> Earth to the sky? What is under my hands,
> That I cannot feel?
>
> What loads my hands down?

The language and the point of view of the poem are clearly his own. He has called his point of view "vivacious melancholy."

A number of poems bear on the search for a sense of significant being, but shadowing all experience, making it heavy, is a sense of time and death, as an undertow. An example is "Next, Please," the final stanza of which contains what may well be one of the most finely wrought images of death in all of English poetry:

*Always too eager for the future, we*
*Pick up bad habits of expectancy.*
*Something is always approaching; every day*
Till then *we say.*

*Watching from a bluff the tiny, clear*
*Sparkling armada of promises draw near.*
*How slow they are! And how much time they waste*
*Refusing to make haste!*

*Yet still they leave us holding wretched stalks*
*Of disappointment, for, though nothing balks*
*Each big approach, leaning with brasswork prinked,*
*Each rope distinct,*

*Flagged, and the figurehead with golden tits*
*Arching our way, it never anchors; it's*
*No sooner present than it turns to past.*
*Right to the last*

*We think each one will heave to and unload*
*All good into our lives, all we are owed*
*For waiting so devoutly and so long.*
*But we are wrong:*

*Only one ship is seeking us, a black-*
*Sailed unfamiliar, towing at her back*
*A huge and birdless silence. In her wake*
*No waters breed or break.*

The poem opens in what seems a not too promising
way. It is in a low key, and the reader readies himself
for the usual lifting of commonplace phrases into a
slightly higher register. In the second stanza the figure
of the ship as promises is introduced, and each stanza
develops it a bit further. The concluding lines of each
stanza have an air of authority, as though our rational
selves were in control of our hopes. Then with the final stanza comes the reversal, the peripety, for we see

that the ship is death. The movement from the com-
monplaces of the opening lines, through the cleverness
and rationality of the middle stanzas, to the grandly
imagined scene of the conclusion presents an ironic,
somewhat complex view of death, death against the
background of everyday preoccupations and illusions.
When critical doctrines stressing order, neatness and
understatement enable a poet to achieve such a quiet
grandeur, then presumably both the doctrines and the
poet deserve attention.

First, the doctrine. In the preface to his section in
*Poets of the 1950's*, Larkin says he avoids theories
about poetry, believing that any abstract notions
might interfere with his writing poems. The doctrine
none the less is there, some of it explicitly stated by
Larkin, as when he says he "has no belief in 'tradition'
or a common myth-kitty or casual allusions in poems
to other poems or poets." Larkin shies away from "big
subjects" and from the lofty manner. It is an axiom
with him that great expectations can come to little and
that the rhetoric usually attending them is pretentious.
A fairly typical poem is "Born Yesterday (for Sally
Amis)":

> *Tightly-folded bud,*
> *I have wished you something*
> *None of the others would:*
> *Not the usual stuff*
> *About being beautiful,*
> *Or running off a spring*
> *Of innocence or love—*
> *They will all wish you that,*
> *And should it prove possible,*
> *Well, you're a lucky girl.*
>
> *But if it shouldn't, then*
> *May you be ordinary;*

> *Have, like other women,*
> *An average of talents:*
> *Not ugly, not good-looking,*
> *Nothing uncustomary*
> *To pull you off your balance,*
> *That, unworkable itself,*
> *Stops all the rest from working.*
> *In fact, may you be dull—*
> *If that is what a skilled,*
> *Vigilant, flexible,*
> *Unemphasized, enthralled*
> *Catching of happiness is called.*

There are the casual phrases from ordinary conversation—"the usual stuff," "you're a lucky girl," and "pull you off your balance." All is held in position by the conviction that happiness may be preferable to brilliance and sparkle.

Perhaps there is a paradoxical situation in the fact that Larkin's negativism or damp enthusiasms are expressed in such neat verse forms. "Reasons for Attendance," to take an example, sets up an opposition between those who find their happiness in romantic love and those who find it in their individual pursuits ("Art, if you like"). It ends:

> *But not for me, nor I for them; and so*
> *With happiness. Therefore I stay outside,*
> *Believing this; and they maul to and fro,*
> *Believing that; and both are satisfied,*
> *If no one has misjudged himself. Or lied.*

The phrases balance each other, and the rhymes build toward an effective dry conclusion. It has the neatness of an expertly organized essay in verse. In the preface, Larkin says he believes the instinct to preserve is behind all art. Possibly a clue to Larkin's neatness is that his is an ironic mind, and the ironist commonly seeks both order and terseness.

Larkin's development has been toward neatness, irony, and an interesting use of commonplace idioms. In *The North Ship*, the stance is that of the Young Poet looking at a romantic landscape. Thus

> *In the field, two horses,*
> *Two swans on the river,*
> *While a wind blows over*
> *A waste of thistles*
> *Crowded like men:*
> *And now again*
> *My thoughts are children*
> *With uneasy faces*
> *That awake and rise*
> *Beneath running skies*
> *From buried places.*

Throughout *The Less Deceived* the tone is ironic and the language is his own. A nice example of his use of commonplace phrases—Auden may have been an influence here—is in "Poetry of Departures":

> *Sometimes you hear, fifth-hand,*
> *As epitaph:*
> He chucked up everything
> And just cleared off,
> *And always the voice will sound*
> *Certain you approve*
> *This audacious, purifying,*
> *Elemental move. . . .*
>
> *So to hear it said*
> He walked out on the whole crowd
> *Leaves me flushed and stirred,*
> *Like* Then she undid her dress
> *Or* Take that you bastard;
> *Surely I can, if he did?*
> *And that helps me stay*
> *Sober and industrious.*

Larkin's metaphors are often quietly effective, and poems manage to be more memorable than phrase by phrase they give promise of being.

G. S. Fraser says that Larkin exemplifies "everything that is good in this 'new movement' and none of its faults." Most of the reviewers of *The Less Deceived* have tagged him as the best of its poets. A few have said he is the best poet of his generation. This is all high praise. It is undoubtedly true that Larkin is a distinguished poet. The range of his subject matter, however, is narrow. Faded photographs, wrong choices, expectations that came to little—this is the sort of thing that engages him. And the wry observation is his usual way of viewing them, although on rare occasions, as in "Toads," he can be rather funny. He has neither Hardy's grim glee nor Housman's ironic hopelessness. He lacks not merely gaudiness but exuberance and open excitement. Traditionally the ambitious poems have been given the higher places in the hierarchy of English poetry—but modest poems also have their place.

# 3    JOHN WAIN:
## THE WILL TO WRITE

REVIEWERS and critics who concern themselves with the health of literature, the future of the novel, with the young poets who give promise of taking a place among the great names in English poetry have an interesting problem in John Wain, novelist, poet, critic, and manifesto writer. He has written four novels, two volumes of poetry, a volume of criticism, a collection of short stories, and innumerable articles, but anyone investigating his work is likely to have a difficult time "placing" him. The novels indicate talent but are also curiously stilted, as though they had been willed into existence, the poems are clever after the manner of Empson, and the criticism while striving for jauntiness and facility is often stiffly academic.

Various theories suggest themselves. Wain began as an academic and appears to be working hard to get over what he considers the debilitating influences that has on anyone with a truly creative drive or talent. This may be a part of his problem. He seems also not to have found his subject matter, or if he has found it not to be quite sure what he sees in it; he has not grappled with it. His contribution to the "new hero" novel, which brought him to public attention, is an historical accident. It is not a subject. And he seems to be searching for his own manner, his own stance, his own style. The search for a subject and the search for one's own "vision" are of course intimately related. All of this implies that a question mark has to be put after Wain's name in any list of the more promising English writers. But of course putting a question mark does not mean he is *not* going to "make it."

Richard Hoggart, in a review of Wain's *Preliminary Essays* (1957) for the *Nation*,[1] attempts to make a judgment about John Wain's achievements in relation to those of other members of the group:

> Of them all, John Wain is the most frequent, fluent and varied publicist. His two novels do not display the imaginative power of Iris Murdoch's or the comic sense of Kingsley Amis', but they are interesting contributions in the new picaresque mode. His "New Academic" poems are sometimes wittily effective, though he cheerfully waives his claims to a leading place as a poet of this kind in favor of Philip Larkin. His criticism is not as promisingly searching as that of Donald Davie, but is more widely engaged, often ranges outside the somewhat restricted field of 'lit. crit.'

But then he adds:

> This collection of essays strengthens one's hunch that just there—in the range of his intelligent hospitality— may be John Wain's real strength. He seems most likely, of any of his generation, to become that valuable and now rare person, the general man of letters.

Possibly Hoggart is right, and Wain is destined to be one of those rare persons, a general man of letters. Wain is still very young, and perhaps no one should try to predict what his role may be. On the other hand, there may be some value in speculating on what Hoggart may have had in mind.

John Wain, like Edmund Wilson, would seem to

be the prototype of the contemporary man of letters. He has as indicated above written poetry, fiction, criticism, essays on matters of cultural interest, and edited a number of literary texts. He also has a very considerable talent for literary journalism. And he has done some editing, both of books and with "First Reading" for the B.B.C. His book reviewing, in *The Spectator*, *Twentieth Century*, the Sunday *Observer* and elsewhere, has been devoted rather strictly to poetry and fiction. His tone has tended to be polemical. He has also interviewed eminent literary figures for the *Observer*, which for a newspaper publishes rather highbrow literary articles and reviews, and of necessity these articles partly turn on the biography of the subject. Possibly this latter sort of writing will serve to make Wain less preoccupied with the ways in which *his* generation has freed English literature. With a more catholic view of the literary situation he might become, as Hoggart suggests, a general man of letters. In the bulk of his work thus far, Wain seems a bright, hard-working young man "turning out" short stories, novels, articles, manifestoes, and poems.

*ii*

There is a common misunderstanding, Wain says, about his background and education. He was not a "scholarship-boy." He did attend the local grammar school at Stoke-on-Trent and therefore is often described as "a typical product of the educational ladder, the poor boy who worked his way up by scholarships and consequently has a fiercely hungry, get-on or get-out attitude." He describes himself as a "recalcitrant and possibly backward" student. None of his teachers ever suggested that he try for a scholarship. He went to Oxford because he wanted to go, and his father, a dentist, paid his way.

Stoke-on-Trent, where Wain was born in 1925, is the city described in Arnold Bennett's *The Old Wives' Tale*. It is also the setting for Wain's *The Contenders*. His father had one of the best practices in the Midlands, and missed being Lord Mayor only because of a technicality. The household was not especially bookish, "although we always had plenty of discussion of general ideas and the house was well stocked with books." Visitors included "local big-wigs, parsons, etc." He describes his family experiences as "quite educative and massively respectable." And he adds that there was a good pipe-line to the working-class too, via the side of the family that had not risen in the world but had remained what the Wains for generations had been, and what their name implies, artisans. Wain says that economically his own path since leaving Oxford has been downward.

Wain knew Amis and Larkin at St. John's Oxford, but they were not "undergraduates together" in the ordinary sense. In 1943 Wain was turned down by the army, and decided to go to Oxford. "It was a bye-term (January 1943). Larkin, who had been rejected earlier, was in his last few weeks before taking his B.A. and going down." Amis was not there at all—he was in the army. During Wain's undergraduate years (1943–46), Amis and Larkin paid occasional visits to St. John's. Wain says he did not realize that Amis had any ambitions as a writer. "He was a marvelous raconteur and joker, and it never struck me he wanted to be anything else." Wain knew however that Larkin was writing both poetry and fiction. He sums up their relationships by saying that while he knew Amis and Larkin he did not count them among his close friends. Nor does he believe he influenced or was influenced by either of them.

Wain stayed on at St. John's as a Fireday Research

Fellow in English, 1946–49. He had made an excellent record as a student, taking a first. Next, he was a Lecturer in English at Reading University but resigned in December 1955. He says he found it increasingly difficult to work both as an academic and as a writer. There is an obvious academic cast to Wain's work, the poetry and fiction as well as the criticism. It could well be true, however, that the academic side of his mind was in conflict with the more creative side—and that his writing thus far shows an effort to unburden himself from the academic.

### iii

Wain's poems have been published in two volumes, *Mixed Feelings* (1951) [2] and *A Word Carved on a Sill* (1956). [3] Wain admires "poise, coherence, and a logical *raison d'être*" in a poem. He finds these characteristics in Empson and in Robert Graves. He does not find them in Auden, Spender, nor in the poets of the 1940's. And there is undoubtedly a family resemblance between his poems and those of Empson and Graves, although neither of the latter seems eager to be credited with having fathered Wain or any of his group. Wain's poetry, as well as his criticism, undoubtedly served as a check on some earlier excesses. There is nothing inherently poetic about emotional self-dramatization nor impenetrable obscurities. But there are dangers on the other side. Public subjects are not necessarily significant, and clarity is a virtue only when it makes a revelation.

In his "Ambiguous Gifts: Notes on the Poetry of William Empson," Wain discusses Empson's remark that a sort "of puzzle interest is a part of the pleasure you are meant to get from [my] poetry." Wain is a little uneasy about poems as puzzles, but he appears to conclude that the puzzle element does contribute to the "passion, logic and formal beauty" of Empson's poetry.

As poet, Wain aspires to "passion, logic, and formal beauty." In the place of puzzles he gives the reader cleverness—and in turn his critics are made uneasy. G. S. Fraser feels that formulae, "tidy" and "highly intelligent," control the poems. Anne Ridler finds Wain's poems "cleverly organized, sometimes witty" —but she concludes that the total effect is "rather dreary." Cleverness, to be admired, should not force itself on a reader's attention. Unfortunately Wain's cleverness, like Empson's puzzles, is inseparable from even his more successful poems.

One of his favorite devices is using arresting lines as a refrain. Such lines "work" when the success of the poem depends upon wittiness. A good example of this is "Gentleman Aged Five before the Mirror":

> *It tells you what you do but never why,*
> *Your image in the glass that watches you:*
> *You cannot catch it napping if you try.*
>
> *It can be counted on to laugh or cry,*
> *Make faces, dance, do anything you do;*
> *It tells you what you do but never why.*
>
> *It is no use to tell the glass a lie;*
> *It answers just as if your words were true.*
> *You cannot catch it napping if you try.*
>
> *Suppose you cross your heart and hope to die,*
> *It silently replies,* I hope so too.
> *It tells you what you do but never why.*
>
> *They say there is a mirror in the sky,*
> *That looks not only at you but right through;*
> *You cannot catch it napping if you try.*

*And yet, it seems, that mirror is too high*
*For you to see however tall you grew,*
*And so you still know What but never Why.*

*You cannot see that mirror till you die.*
*Till then this one will keep you still in view.*
*You cannot catch it napping if you try.*
*It tells you what you do but never why.*

They work less well, if at all, where wittiness is not called for. An instance of this is in "When It Comes," where pathos is the dominant emotion:

*I hope to feel some pity when it comes,*
*Before the burning instant that devours,*
*Before the final flash when terror numbs.*

*Time to seek out a field with grass and flowers*
*And minutes eat like cherries, one by one,*
*Will be my single prayer to those grim Powers.*

*Much that I loved will have already gone—*
*Shapes, places, people, words—but there will be*
*Regret for nothing that has once been done,*

*Because completeness needs no sympathy.*
*If there are tears in that last hour of life*
*Keep them for toilers cheated of their fee.*

*I hope to feel some pity when the knife*
*Plunges at last into the world's sick heart*
*And stills its pounding and its seething strife:*

*Mainly for those who never got a start;*
*The painter with his colours in his head,*
*The actor hoping for a speaking part,*

*The young who leave their proper words unsaid.*
*When all the mountains crash like kettledrums,*
*The hour before my world and I are dead.*

*I hope to feel some pity when it comes.*

"I hope to feel some pity, when it comes," suggests a young poet more concerned with striking an attitude than with the terror implicit in his subject.

Wain belittles certain scholarly interests and methods, and apparently finds most scholars either natively dull or deadened by their pursuits. His own *Contemporary Reviews of Romantic Poetry* (1955) [4] is carefully edited and makes a useful reference work. Another of his academic exercises was the editing of *Interpretations* (1955),[5] an anthology of articles analyzing difficult poems. But there is a scholarly manner that annoys Wain, and he introduces a tone of his own to answer it. One finds sentences like these: "I don't think Professor Knights need feel that he should climb down in deference to *these* arguments," or "Give me Professor Dobrée," or "Dorimant, in his relationship with women, has the fighter-pilot's mentality," or " 'The murder of classical education,' a modern sage has remarked, 'was an inside job.' " Wain is much more at home writing for the critical than for the scholarly journals, and especially for journals edited by nonacademics.

The contributors to *Intrepretations* are "young," and Wain says the generation immediately back of his established this mode of criticism. "They established the right to *be* critics, to talk about a poem without going to either of the extremes; on the one hand, of merely heaping up facts about it, on the other, of merely describing its effect on themselves. Thanks to them, a man writing an analysis of a single poem is not thought to be acting queerly; if he comes under fire, it will be because his analysis appears wrong, not because he ought not to be doing it in the first place." Clearly Wain's generation has been to school to Empson's generation. His own contribution to the volume is an analysis of "Among School

Children." It is especially useful in showing how the first four stanzas are the "actualization of the concepts" stated explicitly in the second four stanzas.

Wain's better criticism appears in *Preliminary Essays*.[6] His quarrel with academic life runs through at least two of them, "Housman" and "The Literary Critic in the University." In the former, he says that until very recently the only don to write vitally imaginative literature was Lewis Carroll (and possibly Walter Pater). The reason for this, he says, is a conflict between professor and poet: the professor who is a poet finds his colleagues sneering at him for being a poet and his nonacademic literary friends sneering at him for being an academic. The poet needs *"luxe, calme, volupté, ordre,* and *beauté,* and all the university can supply him with (perhaps fortunately) is *ordre* and a certain amount of *calme."* He says that Housman solved the problem by assimilating the poet into the professor, and he "proves" this by observing that Housman never admitted any new light and never developed. Wain appears to be playing with words and rationalizing his own situation. In America, John Crowe Ransom and Robert Penn Warren, to single out only two, have been able to accommodate their poetry to their profession as professors or vice versa. And in England, the very group that Wain is associated with are for the most part university lecturers or closely associated with academic life. Wain also oversimplifies the situation of modern literature in the university in "The Literary Critic in the University." The don, he says, snipes at modern literature because he sees himself as the defender of tradition and decorum. Some academics do snipe, but Wain should acknowledge that many excellent critical and scholarly studies of modern literature are written by academics. Nor is the chief argument of the essay very compelling.

Wain is not happy about critical method being taught to undergraduates; undergraduates, he says, are not mature enough to write critical papers and should be taught "facts." One can reply that everything depends on what is meant by "critical method," and "critical papers." If it is true that undergraduates cannot be taught to read more acutely and to state their observations in an orderly way then there is no point in their studying literature at all. Facts about literature can be read in a handbook.

At least two of these essays, "Restoration Comedy and Its Modern Critics" and "Ovid in English," have the look of refurbished "papers" done as course or term assignments. They show that Wain as a student was an acute reader, and knew how to find all the relevant secondary sources. But the fact seems to be that academic life was not Wain's dish of tea.

One of his real talents is for writing essays on his contemporaries or on writers whose work has a bearing on the work of his generation. A good example of the latter is "The Quality of Arnold Bennett." All of us, Wain says, have been overawed by Mrs. Woolf's dismissal of Bennett and "infantile realism" in her "Mr. Bennett and Mrs. Brown" (1924), a plea for a new convention, one allowing for the recognition that "life is a luminous halo, a semi-transparent envelope surrounding us from the beginning of consciousness to the end." Wain is certainly right in saying that Mrs. Woolf's new convention has its own limitations.

*The Years* is an attempt in the same direction as *The Old Wives' Tale,* but can we honestly say that it is equally successful? In stressing the falsity of the accumulated realist method, Mrs. Woolf was not, one feels, allowing sufficient importance to the work done by the reader. The right kind of reader can extract a rich poetic experience from the heaviest and most matter-of-fact compilation, *so long as it is honest*; in fact, it is easier to respond richly to this kind than to the over-lush imaginative novel that provides your poetry for you.

Wain places Bennett in the tradition of Defoe, where he undoubtedly belongs. It is an interesting ascription because his own fiction owes something to the Defoe line.

Wain's views on several modern poets, Pound, Empson, Auden and Thomas, also seem dependent on the way each as an individual contributes or fails to contribute to the kind of verse Wain writes or admires. He does not quote Pound's famous dictum, "Poetry should be at least as well written as prose," but clearly this sort of thing is behind his approval of Pound; he likes Pound's insistence that poets keep language clear and vigorous. He admires Empson's ability to express complex ideas in tight metrical forms. He disapproves of Auden on two grounds: his renunciation of his English citizenship, and his glibness. He sees Thomas as an eccentric genius who managed to rise superior to the visceral and wildly verbal romanticism of the 1940's.

Wain shares his generation's admiration of George Orwell.[7] He tries to say what "kind" of criticism Orwell wrote and to assess its value. The thesis is stated in these sentences: "He was a novelist who never wrote a satisfactory novel, a literary critic who never bothered to learn his trade properly, a social historian whose history was full of gaps. Yet he matters. For *as polemic* his work is never anything less than magnificent; and the virtues which the polemic kind demands—urgency, incisiveness, clarity and humor—he possessed in exactly the right combination."

In discussing Orwell's essay on *Lear*, he shows that Orwell completely missed the point of the multiple plots but adds that he saw the general "message" and was able to relate it at any number of points to human life. Wain says the question of Orwell's literary stature must await a later judgement, the present problem being an exposition of his political ideas. He finds these ideas to be "of the simplest" and "undisguisedly ethical." Anyone, he says, who has read Orwell knows he hated oppression of all kinds, regardless of their source, and that he was good at getting under many of the pretentions to virtue of liberalism in the 1930's and 1940's. All of this is to the good. But Orwell was also capable of saying that he hated "all the smelly little orthodoxies which are now contending for our souls," a statement Wain quotes with approval. Orwell was the outsider, the gadfly. However useful the type is, his contempt usually has a way, and Orwell is no exception, of making the sneer his chief expression. There is little if any affection in Orwell. Whatever delight there is, is a delight in unmasking conscious and unconscious pretensions. Wain is quite good at pointing up Orwell's virtues as a polemicist; he has nothing to say about his vices.

Wain's pronouncements about the poetry written by his group have been frequent. Among the most informative of them is "English Poetry: The Immediate Situation." [8] After rehearsing the history of twentieth-century poetry, he explains the way in which those in the group do cohere:

Round about 1950 a few isolated and very young poets discovered that their tastes coincided. To be precise, they were united more by their dislikes than by their likes. But a broad similarity emerged, and began to show itself in their work. For a brief moment, there *was* a "movement" and it *did* cohere. Then, as always happens, each moved away on his own path, and the moment of coherence was gone. All that remained was a broadly conceived alliance. The poems of, say, Donald Davie do not really resemble those of Philip Larkin or

Kingsley Amis. They only resemble them as compared
with the poems of, say, W. S. Graham. It is one of
those broad concepts, like nationality. A Somerset farm
labourer and a Lancashire miner do not seem to resemble each other until you compare them with a Frenchman—*any* Frenchman.

Common among these poets, he says, is respect for
bed-rock honesty and a dislike of attitudinizing. Not
all of them are practicing critics but without exception they bring a critical consciousness to the writing
of their poems. Wain believes it is no accident that
almost all good English poets have been critics. The
essay as a whole is a plea for well-made poems.

Some of Wain's more recent magazine and newspaper criticism is less polemical and doctrinaire than
his earlier work. For example, "Pseudo-Classic? No,"
a short piece in the *Observer*,⁹ is a relaxed investiga-
tion of *Wuthering Heights*. Wain makes some interesting points, especially those in which he shows
that the novel has a play-like structure, reminiscent
of "the border ballad if not that of Greek tragedy,"
and observes that the novel is "the work of a major
poet." This piece suggests that Wain can write highly
perceptive and disinterested criticism. But the bulk
of the evidence thus far suggests that Wain has not
fully found himself in criticism. There is nothing
wrong about his efforts to criticize earlier writers in
the light of his own commitments—Eliot and others
have done the same thing—but Wain has been given
to oversimplifying issues and taking a too-insistent
tone. His criticism, at least his earlier criticism, could
stand a little more *calme* and a little more *luxe*.

### iv

Wain is commonly credited with being the
first to create a "new hero," Charles Lumley in *Hurry*

*On Down* (1953).[10] Larkin's John Kemp, in *Jill*, had
at least one of the elements of the new hero—inability
to adjust himself to a world he was lifted into thanks
to his education. But critics and reviewers did not
perceive a composite figure until Wain's Lumley had
been joined by Amis' Jim Dixon and Miss Murdoch's
Jake Donahue. The educations of Charles Lumley,
Jim Dixon and Jake Donahue serve to make it harder
for them to "find themselves."

*Hurry On Down* is a satiric novel about a young
man whose bourgeois upbringing and University education have not prepared him for making a satisfactory
living. He feels himself a captive of his training—and
he tries to free himself. The novel concerns itself with
his struggle for freedom. In "Along the Tightrope,"
his contribution to *Declarations* (1958), Wain spells
out the theme:

> An artist can only have one principle: to treat whatever
> seems to him to present itself insistently for treatment,
> in the bits of life lived by him, in the corner of history
> and geography he inhabits. Thus, when I wrote *Hurry
> On Down*, the main problem which had presented it-
> self in my own existence was the young man's problem
> of how to adapt himself to 'life,' in the sense of an order
> external to himself, already there when he appeared on
> the scene, and not necessarily disposed to welcome him;
> the whole being complicated by the fact that in our
> civilization there is an unhealed split between the edu-
> cational system and the assumptions that actually un-
> derlie daily life. We spend a good deal of money, both
> publicly and as individuals, on having the young taught
> to appreciate the masterpieces of literature and art; we
> maintain professors to lecture to them on philosophy
> and other high-flying subjects; and then we turn them
> out into a world that has no use for these things, a
> world whose operative maxim is 'Don't respect or con-
> sider anything except material powers and possessions.'

The basic theme then is that an English liberal education is a poor preparation for getting on in the world.

Essentially *Hurry On Down* is a series of loosely strung together adventures. Individually the adventures do little or nothing to illuminate the theme. Lumley, incidentally, was only a mediocre student, and he has no special talents. Therefore, neither the adventures nor the central character seem designed to test the thesis. The novel as a whole seems rather pointless and inert. Presumably *Hurry On Down* would have been enlivened if the theme had really functioned. It is not surprising that a reader finds both the characters and incidents a little hard to remember.

There is, throughout *Hurry On Down*, a wide-ranging satire on various English types—and this gives the novel whatever interest it has. A second theme, according to Wain, is "the disappearance of the old-style *bourgeoisie*, among whom the hero was supposed to have been brought up." (Wain adds that the hero was widely taken to be a scholarship boy. This, he says, was borrowed from the current excitement about Angry Young Men.) But the ordinary reader will find himself looking hard to discover very much about the disappearance of a class. On the other hand, he will see that Wain is apparently sympathetic with certain working class types, men who know the boundaries of their lives and learn how to live decently within these boundaries.

As the novel opens, Lumley is having trouble with his landlady—she suspects that he has no prospects and is therefore worried about his not being able to pay his rent. Lumley decides to visit Sheila, his fiancée. Arriving at her residence, he learns Sheila is away. But Edith Tharkles, her sister, is there, and so is her stuffy husband, Robert. Both are hostile to him. He insults them—and concludes his visit by showering them with greasy water. He gets drunk in a pub and becomes violently sick. He is now ready for a completely different way of life.

Lumley's first job is as a window cleaner. During this period he lives in a ramshackle building with Edwin Froulish, a self-advertising pseudo-modernist writer, and Betty, a slatternly prostitute who supports Froulish. Lumley takes up a partnership with Ern Ollershaw, who is quiet about his past. Lumley's days are regularized, and his life is painless. Then he sees a girl, Veronica, and falls in love with her. Veronica lives with Mr. Roderick, her "uncle." If Lumley is to have her, he will have to earn more money. At about this stage, Ern Ollershaw is arrested for a part he had played in a car theft racket. Through Ollershaw, Lumley gets into the racket. Adventures of the sort one can see in grade B movies follow—and Lumley lands in the hospital. While there he learns that Veronica is Roderick's mistress.

Lumley then becomes an orderly in the hospital. He takes up with Rosa, a pleasant but rather simple-minded girl. For a short time he believes he will marry her, but he comes to recognize that their interests are too far apart. Meanwhile he has met Mr. Braceweight, a millionaire, and his next job is as Braceweight's chauffeur. The new tutor for Braceweight's son is George Hutchins, a former classmate of Lumley's. The two do not get on well, and Hutchins contributes to Lumley's leaving, or if not specifically to the leaving at least to the way in which he leaves.

Lumley's next job is as a bouncer in a night club. This is followed by a job as a gag writer for a radio show. At this point, Veronica shows up. Lumley still loves her but recognizes that she is the form his new captivity will take, his new cage. "It was dusk now. He crossed the room and turned a switch. The light sprang suddenly into every corner, dramatizing each outline, emphasizing the shape of the furniture and the shape of their predicament." Thus Lumley—and his future.

Wain is pretty good at inventing incidents, working out connections between them, and tying them together. He also writes an intelligent, clean prose. *Hurry On Down*, however, seems to have been willed. One finds it hard to believe that Wain felt compelled to write it. His characters are not memorable, and his events seem not to have been caused but merely to have happened. The reason for the latter probably is that the novel has no significant inner-life.

*Living in the Present* (1955) [11] is also a picaresque satire. Wain, in "Along the Tightrope," has written humbly both about his intentions and the novel's failure to find an audience:

> [It] was meant to be constructive, and to attack fashionable despair and nihilism; the man decides to commit suicide on the first page, and on the last he looks back and wonders how he could have been so misguided; life intervenes and teaches him the necessary lessons. The failure of this book was so spectacular that I can only assume that everyone found it literally unreadable; certainly very few of the comments it received were any use to me, because they all seemed to be by people who had not read further than the first ten pages: e.g. one journalist quite recently attacked the book as 'hysterical,' because it gave a picture of contemporary young manhood as seedy, despairing, self-lacerating, etc.: he should have made it clear that he was talking about the first chapter and letting it stand for the whole, a procedure which, if generally adopted, would revolutionize criticism. There is nothing one can do about this, except admit that the book failed to reach an audience, and write it off.

*Living in the Present* is dull, and the basic reason for this, it would seem, is that Wain lacks the proper touch for what he was trying to write.

Edgar Banks, a school teacher, is bored with life and decides to kill himself. To leave the world a little better, he plans to kill Rollo Philipson-Smith, a man with a storm-trooper mentality and an agent in a totalitarian "Movement." His first attempt to kill Philipson-Smith fails, and he trails him and his foolish Scotch follower McWhirter to Switzerland. In Switzerland he makes further unsuccessful attempts to kill him. These seem somehow lifted from Sherlock Holmes' stories. Banks meets "life" in the form of Mr. and Mrs. Crabshaw and their children, an English family moving to Geneva to improve their standard of living, and Mirabelle, an American journalist, who goes to bed with him but fails to rid him of his twin obsessions, murder and suicide. This remains for another woman to achieve. The other woman is Catherine, the fiancée of Tom Straw, an old friend of his. Banks falls in love with Catherine. Believing he cannot have her, he returns to England. Soon Catherine joins him. It develops that Catherine does not really love Tom, and is thus free to return Banks' love, and that Tom does not love her either. Relief is general and to add to his good fortune Banks gets back his school job. The nihilist had begun to live when he had decided to kill himself. He learns how to engage life and finally to affirm it.

The situation Wain develops, or rather his treatment of it, stresses the preposterous. He uses farce and melodrama, mostly the latter. But something has gone wrong. Possibly it is that the conception asks that an air of unreality be pervasive and constant, and Wain's imagination as a novelist has not been up to the demands.

There are a few funny scenes, especially those showing Mrs. Crabshaw "protecting" her family. The farcical scenes, some of them deliberately vulgar, do not come off. Rollo Philipson-Smith as a neo-fascist has appeared so many times in fiction and in drama and movies that he seems made of cardboard. Catherine, Tom, and several of the lesser characters do exist, but Edgar Banks does not. One feels neither his nihilism nor his affirmation—and without him the whole conception refuses to hold firm.

*Living in the Present* is more clearly a failure than *Hurry On Down*. Both novels cause one to suspect that Wain's creative gifts are not in fiction, at least not in this kind of wildly unrealistic novel carrying an undercurrent of seriousness. At this stage of his career as a novelist, he seemed to lack a sure sense of tone.

In reviewing Wain's third novel, *The Contenders* (1958),[12] John Davenport makes a good point about the way in which critics and reviewers have linked Amis and Wain. "It happened that Wells and Bennett were linked together in the public critical mind, and it has happened to Wain and Amis." He sees Amis as a kind of Wells, bouncy and self-confident, and Wain as a Bennett, drawing on his Midland common-sense "to produce a happy ending smooth as Hanley pot." Mr. Davenport says *The Contenders* is similar to one of Bennett's light-hearted card tricks. The comparison of Wells and Bennett with Amis and Wain can be carried even further. Amis is essentially a comic satirist. Wain is a satirist too, but the moralist is very strong in him. This becomes evident in *The Contenders*, and with the benefit of hindsight, one can see that the strain of down-to-earth morality is what Wain was searching for in his earlier fiction.

Wain spells out the theme of *The Contenders* early in the first chapter. Briefly, the English school system, especially from the Sixth Form on, demands such intense competition that the young are marked by it, and some of them spend their entire lives pursuing goals the inherent value of which they never question.

What most of the Sixth were after, says the narrator, Joe Shaw, was a scholarship to Oxford or Cambridge. Shaw "dropped out, right at the beginning, and said that the Higher Cert. was good enough for me and they could keep Oxford and Cambridge." Neither of his two friends, Ned Roper, a businessman, and Robert Lamb, an artist, go beyond the Higher Certificate either—but both were careerists. Their competition took the form of Ned's trying to become Robert's patron, to make him dependent, and Robert's trying to owe nothing to him, and, more important, each trying to win Myra, a beautiful but empty-headed creature whose fate it was to walk on the arm of "successful" men. Ned takes Myra away from Robert, and the latter turns to Pepina, a faithful and loving Italian girl. But before long Robert leaves her and goes off in pursuit of Myra. Joe Shaw, the only one of the three men who knows true value when he sees it, falls in love with Pepina.

The theme is kept in focus chapter by chapter—and there is never any doubt about what the point of the novel is. But somehow, the story *approaches* allegory. Joe Shaw is the Thoughtful Man, Ned is the Businessman Careerist, Robert the Artist Careerist, Myra the Beautiful Symbol of Success, and Pepina is True Value. As a kind of morality play, *The Contenders* is interesting.

As a novel, it is deficient, although not entirely, in characterization. Ned is always neat, self-controlled, and determined; Robert is talented, explosive, and egotistical; and Myra is mindless beauty. They serve the plot—the plot does not afford them a chance to grow or change. They are fixed and not quite believable. Joe is more believable—he analyzes his own motives, he has a rather heavy ironic humor, and at the end his humdrum life picks up excitement. And Pepina is believable. Some of the incidental characters, such as Robert's grandparents, are humorously done—the grandfather as a walrus, the grandmother as a seal; and there are several other good characterizations.

### v

A *Travelling Woman* (1959),[13] may be either a step forward or a step backward for Wain, depending on where one throws the emphasis. In technique, it may be a step forward insofar as he is able to stay with the convention he sets up. In theme, nothing much is achieved, and the reason for this seems to be that at a crucial point he seems to forget the point of his convention.

George Links is a young lawyer, with a wife, Janet, who though pretty enough no longer excites him. Hoping to stir a little fire in him, she suggests he take psychiatric treatments. George has no intention of being analyzed, but he accepts the opportunity of visiting London twice a week for seemingly legitimate reasons. He finds quarters in the house of the Cowleys, and soon is having a passionate affair with Ruth Cowley. Janet learns about this and, in turn, has an affair with Captax, the friend of George who had got him a room at the Cowleys. There is also another couple, Evan and Barbara Bone, friends of Captax. Barbara is attracted to George but he does not reciprocate her feelings. Eventually, after Ruth has broken off with him, George wants to patch things up with Janet, but she, even though she has left Captax, refuses.

The moral appears to be that poor George did not have enough imagination to realize his marital infidelities could lead him and others into situations he had not bargained for. This is a meager enough moral, and hardly a new one. But in reading the novel one is not at all sure that the moral was what Wain had in the forefront of his mind when he began A *Travelling Woman*. The title suggests that the novel is centered on Janet, but of course it is centered on George. If it were on her Wain would have an opportunity to describe the feelings of a "wronged" woman, possibly a more interesting subject than poor George's infidelities, at least as Wain develops them.

There is real confusion too about the convention Wain uses to tell the story because, one, he does not maintain it to the end, and two, he does not develop the theme that the convention seems to promise. The action as a whole is foreshortened, and all moves at a fast clip. The characters are seen in isolation or in small groups as they might be on a sparsely furnished stage—there is no complicated life of the town, city or railroad coach back of them. The writing is intended to be witty and clever and sometimes, not always, it succeeds in being both.

The convention, perhaps borrowed in part from Restoration drama and in part from Wilde or Beardsley, asks that the sex game be seen in all its comic absurdity. Ruth Cowley doesn't like George but she goes to bed with him. When George thinks about her he has no more control over himself than he would if he were falling down a long well in *Alice in Wonderland*. Janet is "right" for George but he doesn't understand that she is. Barbara Bone is attracted to George because of a little game he played with her shoe, and Evan Bone crackles with jealousy as soon as George turns his eyes toward Barbara. If Wain had a theory about all this—about the comic element in sex—the convention would work. But in the final chapters, he seems to forget how witty and brittle and clever he was being, and the action suddenly is resolved in a moralistic way.

Wain seems torn between wanting to be a wit and needing to be a moralist. He ought to make up his mind. And since he is not really a great wit, his choice should not be difficult.

### vi

John Wain's search for a subject has apparently been toward old-fashioned moral truths. The moral issue in *The Contenders* is simple and unsophisticated. In *A Travelling Woman* a moral point is suddenly there in an obtrusive and really unearned way. If Wain is to find a place as a moralist, however, he will have to treat more complicated moral problems. He has the Midlands city that Bennett had as a source for home-grown characters and perennially engaging themes, and there is London and the Continent for contrasts. What is missing thus far is a sense of moral ambiguities.

In "Along the Tightrope," Wain says his first two novels juxtaposed the solemn and the comic—a "mingling of the grotesquely comic with the sombre or even tragic." In his third novel, *The Contenders*, he said he had employed a "compound" of the serious and the comic. It would be interesting to know how he sees the relationship of the comic and the solemn in *A Travelling Woman* as a juxtaposition, a compound or a confusion? The compound, not the juxtaposition, is probably best suited to Wain's talent, which is engaged by sober ethical issues, accompanied by an irony that is a little on the heavy side. It is in the Bennett country that he seems most at home.

*Nuncle*, Wain's first volume of short stories, was published in 1960. It is recognizably the work of the author of *Hurry On Down, Living in the Present*,

*The Contenders*, and *A Travelling Woman*. There is
the same need to experiment, and there is a similar
selecting and forcing of subjects which seem not to
have chosen the writer. The opening story, for example, "Master Richard" sets up a promising situation—the narrator is a young child who has the mind
and the interests of a thirty-five year old man. Certain
writers might have pursued the possibilities in this to
the point where they had either a high comic or painfully grotesque conflict. Wain does not make much
of it, and what begins promisingly trails off inef-
fectually.

The title story "Nuncle" is another matter. Presumably it grows out of a fantasy that must haunt
many writers—the inability to write. The writer in
this story is fifty years old. His first novels made him
famous, but for twenty years he has written nothing.
The action, pathetic and comic, grows out of his effort
to rehabilitate himself and to become productive
again. It carries conviction, and possibly may be read
as Wain's salute to his profession, writing.

## *4* IRIS MURDOCH:
THE FORMAL AND THE
CONTINGENT

IRIS MURDOCH's *Under the Net* was published at about the same time as Amis's *Lucky Jim* and Wain's *Hurry On Down*. Inevitably reviewers saw the three authors as a postwar school of satirists. Miss Murdoch sees slight justification for calling them a school. "About the Wain-Amis business. I know Wain personally. I don't know Amis. I don't think we have any tenets in common, except being all left-wing. I belong to a slightly older generation than Wain and Amis, which gives even our politics a different flavor."

She does admit that Jake Donahue has one tenuous point of resemblance with the early heroes of Amis and Wain—all are raffish and unsettled, and they live in an unsettled world. "But on closer inspection," she says, "I think Jake is very unlike Dixon and Lumley. Jake's ancestors are Beckett's Murphy and Queneau's Pierrot." *Under the Net* is dedicated to Raymond Queneau.

The characters in Beckett's *Murphy* (1938) live in a dim, fey world. Murphy resigns from society, and lives in a rocking chair. The world he inhabits and contemplates has an eerie insubstantiality. The world of *Pierrot Mon Ami* (1943) is particularized and bizarre. Pierrot, a small, ineffectual man, finds that nothing ever quite works out as he had hoped, but he is prepared for adversity, and he has a fine sense of the comic. Much of the action takes place in an amusement park. The characters suit the setting. They indulge in sentimental actions, are carried along by the rhythms of the day or the weather, and most of them survive their big and little problems. Big issues seem either not to exist or to dissolve even as one contemplates them. The characters in *Pierrot* learn to live with and to enjoy the world of particulars.

The world Miss Murdoch created in *Under the Net* is indeed closer to the bizarre world of *Pierrot* than it is to the worlds of *Lucky Jim* or *Hurry On Down*. Miss Murdoch is clearly a francophile, and she admires that literature-philosophy *rapprochement* of the French.

### ii

Miss Murdoch was born in Dublin, in 1919, of Anglo-Irish parents. She grew up in London, and attended a boarding school, Badminton School, Bristol. She read Classical Greats at Somerville College, Oxford, taking her degree in 1942. During the next two years she worked for the British Treasury. From 1944 to 1946 she worked for U.N.R.R.A., mostly in Belgium and Austria. The following year she returned to Oxford as a tutor and fellow in philosophy at St. Anne's. She is married to John Bayley, a novelist and a don at New College. At present she is University Lecturer. She has been a student of "analytical" philosophy, but finds it deficient in dealing with questions of morality[1] or politics—her own special interests. She finds existentialist theories a necessary supplement, although she is not committed to any particular existentialist school. These various experiences and interests turn up in her fiction.

*Under the Net* (1954) ² is pervaded by an air of unreality. Many of the characters either float through their days, live in dreams, or have their being in relationship to that world of studied unreality, the films. The view of the narrator is such that each is surrounded by a little nimbus of pathos. The satire is sympathetic. In the end, at least two of the characters, Jake Donahue and Hugo Belfounder, his philosophical friend, achieve a firmer hold on reality.

Jake Donahue makes his living as a translator and as a writer, doing original work only when he can't do otherwise. A lonely man, he finds companionship in pubs and cafés. Early in the book, he tells about having loved Anna Quentin, a singer, and says he had come close to asking her to marry him. She would have said no, and the marriage probably would not have worked anyway because she took life "intensely and very hard," whereas Jake thinks "it is foolish to take life so, as if you were to provoke a dangerous animal which will break your bones in the end in any case." Donahue lives with Finn, a somber man and a great drinker. They work very hard at getting free quarters, usually in some woman's flat. When the story opens, Donahue and Finn are being asked to leave the attic room they had been occupying. Madge, with whom Donahue had had an affair, now cooled, is taking up with an ex-bookie turned movie producer, Sammy Starfield—and she wants Donahue and Finn to vacate.

This causes Donahue to go in search of Anna, who is running an arty "little theatre" in Hammersmith. When Jake sees Anna, he feels the old warmth toward her. She is delighted to see him but says he cannot take up residence in the theatre. She does allow him to spend one night there, and he goes to sleep, wrapped in a bear's skin, in a room filled with countless objects used at one time or another in the theatre.

Anna has told him that her sister Sadie, a film star, is looking for a caretaker for her apartment, and he decides to apply for the job. Sadie greets him enthusiastically, but he finds her not only catty but a kind of walking mannikin. She gives him the job, which involves "protecting her" from Hugo Belfounder.

Belfounder, we are told, was an old and intimate friend of Jake's. They had held many philosophical discussions. Belfounder had always been able to make a great deal of money, but money does not interest him. Jake had put Belfounder's fascinating talk into a book, *The Silencer*, in the form of a dialogue. Feeling this was a betrayal of his friend and therefore embarrassed, Jake had avoided Belfounder. The book was a failure, and Belfounder, as we learn later, had not even recognized his own words. Belfounder had since become a successful movie producer—and thus his acquaintance with Sadie.

Once established in Sadie's apartment, Jake finds she has locked him in. This frustrates him and he calls on Finn, an expert picker of locks, and Dave, another philosophical friend, to come and let him out. A long trail of pub crawling follows, during which they pick up Lefty, a left-wing political organizer. The day ends with a drunken early-hour swim in the Thames.

Sadie and Sammy—there is a wildly fortuitous meeting of characters throughout the novel—scheme to use one of Jake's translations as the basis for a movie script. This leads Jake and Finn into stealing Mars, an ageing dog who is a movie idol. Meanwhile, also, Jake has decided he must renew his friendship with Hugo Belfounder. He meets Belfounder on a movie set. A political riot breaks out, with fighting all over the movie lot, but Jake, with the assistance of Mars, eludes the police.

Jake is next in Paris, talking to Madge. She is now the mistress of a wealthy man who wants to promote an Anglo-French movie company. Involved in the enterprise is Jean Pierre Breteuil, the second-rate author whose books Jake has regularly translated. Breteuil has just won the Prix Goncourt, and his book *Nous Les Vainqueurs* is to be the basis of their first script. Madge offers Jake a fabulous salary, one, because he is a writer but mostly because she needs him herself. Jake refuses. The following chapter shows Jake searching Paris for Anna, whom he knows to be there. Jake finally sees her, follows her, loses her. There is a will-o'-the-wisp quality to the search.

Back in London, Jake takes a menial job in a hospital. Oddly, Belfounder, victim of a concussion, is brought to the hospital. Jake learns from him that he, Belfounder, had loved Sadie, that Sadie had loved Jake, and that Anna had loved Belfounder. They live in a circle of frustration. Belfounder has decided to become a watchmaker, a job he feels to be worthwhile. He calls it an old trade, like baking bread. Belfounder believes that everyone must have a trade to help him keep going.

Belfounder, at one point, is called "the theme" of *Under the Net,* so presumably he is to be listened to. He tells Jake that some things can't be understood and therefore should be dropped: "One must just blunder on. Truth lies in blundering on." This advice seems to have a connection with the book's title.

A further part of the book's theme is stated in the final chapter:

> Events stream past us like these crowds, and the face of each is seen only for a minute. What is urgent is not urgent forever but only ephemerally. All work and all love, the search for wealth and fame, the search for truth, life itself, are made up of moments which pass

and become nothing. Yet through this shaft of nothings we drive onward with that miraculous vitality that creates our precarious habitations in the past and the future. So we live—a spirit that broods and hovers over the continual death of time, the lost meaning, the unrecaptured moment, the unremembered face, until the final chop-chop that ends all our moments and plunges that spirit back into the void from which it came. [268]

This has an existentialist ring to it. Shortly thereafter, in the company of Mrs. Tinckham, a small shopkeeper who knows how to put up with things and keep going, Jake decides he is through with translating. He determines to be a serious writer. The book ends on the note struck by Hugo Belfounder—that work and creative achievement are an answer to the passage of time, moments not to be recaptured, and lost meanings.

*Under the Net* is filled with absurdity and confusion. It catches a world not so very different from Sartre's world—but in *Under the Net* there is little exacerbation of spirit. Miss Murdoch's world is serious but suffused by a sense of the unaccountable and the ridiculous. Its advice is that one can find satisfaction with the particular.

### iii

Even after several close readings of *The Flight from the Enchanter* (1956), one could find its diverse meanings hard to perceive. On a number of occasions there are statements similar to this: "One reads the signs as best one can, and one may be totally misled. But it's never certain that the evidence will turn up that makes everything plain." Peter Saward, a scholar, says this, but certain other characters might also have said it. Still, much more is going on. One is tempted to say *The Flight from the Enchanter* is like Shakespeare's *The Tempest*. Strange auguries are in the air, and the rules of cause and effect seem suspended. All seems bewitched.

The characters in *The Flight from the Enchanter* know each other, and slip easily and often unexpectedly in and out of one another's rooms or apartments. The action involves factory employees, ambitious white-collar workers, graduates from the ancient universities, wealthy old ladies, and an interesting assortment of the foreign born. It is a cross section of English life.

One is often uncertain about the meaning of a given chapter but the action itself, sharply delineated and often grotesquely comic, almost suffices. The opening chapter presents Annette Cockeyne leaving a fashionable London school. Before leaving, she swings from a chandelier and presents the school with a book from its own library. She goes tripping off down the street toward the home of Rosa Keepe, a friend of Annette's mother.

Rosa is undoubtedly the central figure. She lives with her brother, Hunter, who is the editor of a magazine, *Artemis*. Rosa has declined to marry Mischa Fox but is fascinated by him. She basks in Peter Saward's love but she does not love him. She works in a factory because she feels this gives her a firmer hold on reality. At the factory she has become friendly with two vigorous young Poles, Stephan and Jan Lusiewicz (figures out of Grimm's fairyland). She has taught them English and helped them adapt themselves. Each of the brothers, both unselfcritical male egotists, makes violent love to her, and, as she says, "the mastery passed to them." Their old mother, in an advanced state of physical decay, is present while the love-making goes on. Rosa is attracted to the brothers but afraid their existence will become known to Hunter and her friends. These brothers do intrude into the other side of her life. Jan attempts to attack Annette, and Stephan takes up residence with Rosa and Hunter and sets fire to Hunter's hair when asked to move.

Mischa Fox, at Rosa's request for help, arranges a government order affecting Europeans born east of a certain line—and Stephan disappears. Rosa is again attracted to Mischa and journeys to Italy to join him. But Calvin Blick intimidates her into leaving. For one thing, he has a compromising picture of Rosa and the Polish brothers, and for another, he tells her that the deportation order had caused Nina, Mischa's close friend, to commit suicide. Rosa returns to Peter Saward, offering to marry him, but he declines because he knows she does not love him.

There are a number of wonderfully drawn types in the novel, such as Mrs. Wingfield, John Rainborough, and Miss Casement. Mrs. Wingfield is elderly, eccentric, and wealthy. She delights in saying insulting and disturbing things. John Rainborough, university educated, wants mostly not to be disturbed. The ruthless Miss Casement is a most effective bureaucrat.

Another part of the action includes the magazine, *Artemis*. It had been started by Rosa's mother and other ardent young suffragettes. But over the years its supporters have neglected it and it is on the verge of collapse. Mischa Fox wants to buy it, but Hunter resists. Eventually *Artemis* is saved by Mrs. Wingfield and her elderly contemporaries.

This partial summary of the plot gives no sense of the vitality of the novel, the characterizations, the satire, and the sense of strange jewels that seem to shine in an eerie green light. Nor does it explain the novel as allegory—for it is only as allegory that *The Flight from the Enchanter* makes sense.

The key to the allegory is Mischa Fox. He stands

for the absolutist state. Mischa Fox is a great senti-
mentalist. Thus his love of the people he controls. He
is also capable of great cruelty. He organizes other
people's lives, and many of them are all too willing
to give themselves into his power. Rosa (who incidentally is a Socialist) resists him until he solves the
problem of Stephan. Mischa Fox is willing to use
police state methods to attain his ends, or he is willing
to have his agent, Calvin Blick, use them for him.
Mischa Fox lives in an aura of mystery and grandeur,
a symbol of knowingness and power. But the *Artemis*
episode, with the old ladies gathering their forces to
prevent the sale of the magazine, seems designed to
show that his power can readily be resisted. There is
also a very nice passage near the end of the novel
which says that the liberal tradition in England pre-
vents such inhuman orders as mass deportations, and
adds that if Nina had understood English feelings in
the matter she would not have resorted to suicide.
Mischa Fox's methods and his willingness to play
God pervert even his own good intentions. He is a
wicked Prospero.

The title, *The Flight from the Enchanter*, of course
comes from "Ode to the West Wind":

*O, Wild West Wind, thou breath of Autumn's being,*
*Thou, from whose unseen presence the leaves dead*
*Are driven, like ghosts from an enchanter fleeing. . . .*

There is a wild spirit moving everywhere, destroying
and preserving. In the midst of it all sits Mischa Fox,
the enchanter, a magician who promises to solve all
problems. He is a temptation to be resisted.

### iv

*The Sandcastle* (1957) has none of the demi-
monde strangeness of *Under the Net* and none of the

allegory-in-wonderland quality of *The Flight from the Enchanter*. The mystery and strangeness it does have is the mystery and strangeness of rather ordinary and unspectacular people. The central situation is an old one—a middle-aged man, twenty years married, and with two children nearing university age, falls in love with a young painter and she with him.

Bill Mor is a teacher at St. Bride's, a school near London. He has aspired to run for Parliament on the Labour ticket, but the plan is distasteful to Nan, his wife, and she is determined to thwart him. Mor is the kind who leaves the room rather than have a quarrel —and Nan, unimaginative and determined to have her own way, takes advantage of his good will. Mor loves his son, Donald, and daughter, Felicity, but he does not feel close to them nor they to him. He is an undemonstrative, rather puritanical man, and on one occasion he wonders whether or not he is "real."

Miss Murdoch has her usual colorful *dramatis personae*, all sharply rendered: Demoyte, the retired headmaster, sharp-tongued, generous, and intolerant of incompetents; Everard, Demoyte's successor, well-intentioned, fatuous, and bumbling; Tim Burke, a jeweller, member of the Labour Party, friend of Mor, and in love with Nan; Bledyard, the stammering, pious art teacher, and so on.

Rain Carter, a gifted painter, is at St. Bride's to do a portrait of Demoyte. She is charming; she represents youth, talent, freedom—and Mor falls in love with her. In him she sees the strength and character of her recently dead father. She is concerned about the immorality of breaking up Mor's marriage, but he tells her the marriage was already gone. Nan, discovering them in an early morning embrace, is shocked, but shortly she recovers herself and instructs Mor to put an end to his foolishness before he and the family are made ludicrous. Then she goes off to Dorset with Felicity, fully expecting her orders to be carried out.

A mysterious gypsy links Rain to Felicity. The latter also indulges in magic rites at the sea shore, a symbolic effort to bring her father back to the family. But, by and large, the novel is in the realistic tradition.

Earlier, Rain Carter has explained that on the Mediterranean coast she was never able to make a sturdy, permanent sandcastle—the wind, the rain, the sun, and the very texture of the sand made it impossible. The symbolism is clear enough—Mor and Rain Carter are not going to be able to build a sandcastle. He is determined to marry Rain, but he delays first because Donald has yet to take his entrance exams for the university. Nor has he been able to make his decision known to Nan. Next, Donald is involved in an escapade, climbing the tower at St. Bride's. He is not injured (his companion is); upset, he runs away from home. All this causes Mor to delay acting upon his decision. The final determining incident occurs at the public unveiling of Demoyte's portrait. Nan uses the occasion of a toast to announce to the school that her husband is going to stand for Parliament. Rain had not known about his political ambitions. She now realizes that the direction of his life has already been formed, and decides that their marriage would eventually be unsuccessful. Mor stays with his family, and they take up their lives *almost* as they were before.

At one point the theme is stated explicitly. Freedom has to make terms with necessity. Obviously *The Sandcastle* does not present as wild or as strange a world as those in the first two novels. It has excitement and it is convincing, but in comparison with the earlier novels it wears an air of the commonplace.

*v*

With *The Bell* (1958), her fourth novel in five years, Miss Murdoch emerges as probably the best of the young novelists. There is the same odd assortment of characters, representing a cross section of English life, the action is bathed in an air of unreality but yet seems credible, and there are highly intelligent speculations about human freedom and the nature of the good dexterously woven into action. The philosophical preoccupations of Miss Murdoch's generation, centered around the notion of the free and lonely self, pervade the novel. It is this, more than anything else, that lifts *The Bell* above provinciality, that separates it from the local and temporary English situation.

Her analysis of Imber Court, an agrarian community reminiscent of those desired by Ruskin and Morris, is mercilessly intelligent and yet sympathetic. Imber Court is attached to a covent of cloistered Benedictine Anglican nuns. The Abbess tells Michael Meade, who owns Imber Court, that there are those who can neither live in the world nor out of it. She hopes Imber Court will be the haven for some of them. But Miss Murdoch will not be persuaded. "Those who hope," she says, "by retiring from the world, to earn a holiday from human frailty in themselves and others are usually disappointed." *The Bell* is the complicated story of the disintegration of Imber Court. Each of the characters carries his own weaknesses, neuroses, annoying characteristics, and one of them her madness into the community. There is a suicide and an attempted suicide. The high-minded Michael Meade, the leader of the community, is trapped, when he is least prepared for resistance, by his homosexual tendencies. Imber Court is not free

from bad tempers, stupidity, self-righteousness, jealousy, drunkenness, and sexual temptations of various
sorts. The would-be agrarian simplicity of the community is the ironic backdrop for farcial human actions and moral ambiguities. It takes Imber Court a
year to disintegrate, but toward the end, thanks to
Miss Murdoch's wild inventiveness, events rush in
grotesque helter-skelter toward a complete debacle.

### vi

Miss Murdoch's interest in existentialism is
very clear. Her two B.B.C. talks provide the easiest
introduction to the subject. The first of them is "The
Novelist as Metaphysician." [3] It would not be to the
point here to discuss the antecedents of Sartre's
thought nor the rightness, wrongness, coherence or
incoherence of his doctrines. But a couple of quota-
tions will give us the typical situation of the Sartrean
protagonist. The first is this:

> To get the full flavour of this drama I think that the
> keyword is 'ambiguity.'. . . The free and lonely self,
> whose situation Sartre pictures in these somewhat Kier-
> kegaardian terms, discovers the world to be full of am-
> biguities. These have to be, and are resolved by action.
> . . . That is, we are condemned to choose our religion
> or lack of it, our politics or lack of it, our friends or lack
> of them. Within the wide limits of our historical situa-
> tion we choose one world or another one.

The second is a quotation from A. J. Ayer which Miss
Murdoch says might have come from Sartre:

> 'There is nothing to be done about it, except look at the
> facts, look at them harder, look at more of them, and
> then come to a moral decision. Then asking whether
> the attitude that one has adopted is the right attitude
> comes down to asking whether one is prepared to stand
> by it. There can be no guarantee of its correctness, be-

cause nothing counts as a guarantee. Or rather, something may count for someone as a guarantee, but counting something as a guarantee is itself taking up a moral standpoint.'

Miss Murdoch adds that the isolated self is free to and should make moral decisions, but that no one and no system can guarantee the rightness of the decision.

Passages in "The Existentialist Hero" [4] make all this even clearer. The Marxist, she says, differs from, and distrusts, the existentialist because of the latter's capacity for self-doubt. The Marxist feels that "nature has its own dialectical history, and its own rationally explicable and developing interactions with the activities of man." The existentialist finds nature meaningless and absurd—only he can give it meaning. He tells us that "we are free, and that we enter into a situation which is already partly formed. We must both engage in some consistent course of action, and keep on remembering that nothing guarantees that we are right. The temper required here is heroic."

*Sartre, Romantic Rationalist* [5] is a sympathetic yet critical study of Sartre's philosophy, drama, and fiction. It is a working out in greater detail of the themes developed in the B.B.C. talks. Possibly the most interesting chapter for the reader of Miss Murdoch's own fiction is the final one, "Linguistic Acts and Linguistic Objects."

The chapter discusses Sartre's theory of *la littérature-engagée*, and passes a judgment on his performance as a novelist. The novel, she says, has always been concerned "with people's treatment of each other, and so it is about human values." In other words, the novelist is expected to present human relationships in a "morally mature" way. Sartre's novels are, she says, intensely serious and they are morally mature. "But what about his manner, in the novels, of making his thought concrete?" She believes his characters have the appearance of being moved externally in order to support ideas—"and that the colour is applied to them externally in a decorative manner." Sartre is interested in "essences rather than existences" and in "issues rather than people." His talent is for social diagnosis and for psychoanalysis, especially of grotesques. The rationalist can be a good dramatist, Miss Murdoch says, and she instances Shaw —but rarely is he a good novelist. Sartre is a very good dramatist; he is far from being a great novelist. Miss Murdoch's evaluation of Sartre seems a fair one.

Yet another discussion of the novel, a more ambitious piece, is "The Sublime and Beautiful Revisited," a Bergen lecture at Yale.[6] Miss Murdoch devotes the first half of the essay to conceptions of personality and freedom as these are discussed in post-Renaissance philosophy. In the latter half she discusses the modern Symbolist novel. The center of her argument is that the Symbolist novel, aspiring to be a thing-in-itself, self-contained, denies or tries to purge away contingency:

> One might say of the Symbol that it is an analogon of the individual, but not a real individual. It has the uniqueness and separateness of an individual, but whereas the real individual is boundless and not totally definable, the symbol is known intuitively to be self-contained: it is a making sensible of the idea of individuality under the form of necessity, its contingency purged away. Plato mistrusted art because it imitated what was various and unreal; the symbolists desired an art which would have satisfied Plato. [260]

Miss Murdoch makes the point that the Hulme-Eliot aesthetic, with its emphasis on the self-contained symbol, was a reaction against that part of Romanticism that spoke for the untidy, life-loving Rousseauesque elements. The Hulme-Eliot, or the Symbolist, line influenced the novel, causing it to want to be wholly self-contained. "What is feared is history, real beings, and real change, whatever is contingent, messy, boundless, infinitely particular, and endlessly to be explained; what is desired is the timeless non-discursive whole which has its significance completely contained in itself." She does not ask that the novelist turn his back on form and write journalism; on the other hand, she insists that the novel is not the poem. She believes that the modern emphasis on formal control has worked against both a multiplicity of characters and the multiple aspects of personality. "A novel must be a house fit for free characters to live in; and to combine form with a respect for reality with all of its contingent ways is the highest art of prose."

Miss Murdoch's fiction can be read or interpreted as a willingness or a desire on her part to loosen the claims for the formal, and to allow the contingent, the inexplicable, and the elusive to pass in review. Politically too, she is afraid that excesses of the orderly, the neat, the formal mean the destruction of the rich, the varied, the curious, the eccentric.[7]

Her own fiction is indebted to Sartre or at least presents a view of the human situation very like his. Man, a lonely creature in an absurd world, is impelled to make moral decisions, the consequences of which are uncertain. Unlike Sartre, however, Miss Murdoch can create living characters. Her talent is for evoking the concrete, a sense of mystery, the flow of events. And she has what Sartre lacks completely, a sense of humor.

Many of her more fascinating characters are comic grotesques. She is able to create such characters because she has a fine sense of fantasy and comedy. But they have another reason for existing. The comic grotesques are characters whose creator has refused to submit them to the ordeal of taking on classical forms.

### vii

With her fifth book, A *Severed Head* (1961), Iris Murdoch pretty definitely established the nature of her talent. One can now see more clearly the outline or perimeter of her subject matter, and also perceive the rules followed in putting together a Murdoch novel. *Under the Net* introduced a half-world of writers and actors and left wingers who are out of touch with the mores of both the lower classes and the middle classes. The characters come alive or pursue their dreams most ardently when twilight falls, or most soulfully when the dawn is breaking. There is something touching and pathetic about their lostness. *The Flight from the Enchanter* is an allegorical novel, although the reader is never very certain that each character can be reduced to an abstract meaning; he is satisfied that the over-all intent is allegory. That no one, out of love or weakness, should wholly submit his will to the will of another is the theme. *The Sandcastle* has characters pursuing their dreams, but the environment, a boy's school, and the subject, the strain in the relations of a middle-aged married couple, are not sufficiently bizarre. Miss Murdoch's essentially strait-laced morality needs an amoral world before her wit and eccentric symbols can become radiant. *The Bell* has such an environment and subject. A group of injured and hurt creatures inhabit a religious monastery or retreat—and demonstrate that we carry our injuries and hurts with us, regardless of where we may go.

*The Severed Head* is recognizably an Iris Murdoch novel. Almost without exception the characters are amoral. They too are hurt creatures, while pretending not to be. They inhabit the middle-class intellectual world—have attended or teach at a university. One merchandises excellent wines, all accept psychiatry as a fact of life, some sculpt or paint, one lives on her inheritances, all drink a great deal, and all accept divorces with the ease and grace of buying a sleek new car. It is a world of easy and gracious relationships—and sudden attempts at suicide. Miss Murdoch, as usual, envelopes all this in an aura of eerie reality. If one does not quite know the characters, mostly it is because they have no true identities.

Palmer Anderson, a fifty year old psychiatrist of American origins who rules the little domain of the action, is the essence of assured knowledge, of candid understanding, and of generous, open, easy relationships. He is tall, graceful, masculine, good-looking. He would inhabit and have others inhabit a painless world. Antonia, the wife of Martin Lynch-Gibbon, the narrator, is having an affair with Palmer, her analyst. Martin has also been having an affair with Georgie, a recent university graduate.

Martin has kept his affair secret. Antonia, older than he, has a "mother relationship" with him. In the two women he finds complementary satisfactions. When Antonia tells him she and Palmer want to be married, he is deeply upset. He soon realizes he doesn't want to marry Georgie, and so does Georgie. With a typical Murdoch sort of gesture, Georgie cuts off her hair and mails it in a box to Martin—then attempts suicide. Martin wants to keep his wife, but his "civilized side" wants to let her go since this is her desire. There are a number of chummy scenes in which the three, Palmer, Antonia, and Martin, participate. On

one occasion Palmer and Antonia are in bed together
—while Martin talks with them. Martin's brother,
Alexander, a sculptor, and sister edge in and out of the
main action.

Through the various episodes moves a middle aged
Jewess, Honor Klein, a half sister of Palmer Anderson.
She is reminiscent of Mischa in *The Flight from the
Enchanter*. She is an enchantress, but her role differs
from Mischa's. This is Martin's first impression of
her:

> It was not a very pleasant face: heavy, perceptibly Jew-
> ish, and dour, with just a hint of insolence. The curving
> lips were combined with a formidable straightness and
> narrowness of the eyes and mouth. Dr. Klein advanced
> from the barrier and stood still, looking about. She was
> frowning, and looked haggard in the lurid yellowish
> light. She wore no hat and drops of foggy moisture
> stood already upon her short black hair.

Honor Klein teaches at Cambridge and thus does not
offend unduly against verisimilitude. None the less,
she is a goddess, and hints at dark, primeval and inevitable rituals and actions.

When news of the impending divorce and marriage
reach her she arrives quickly in London. It is not
clear at first whether she will interfere with the marriage. Clearly she disapproves of it. Eventually she
tells Martin "the facts of life": that everything has to
be paid for, including love; no one is helped by being
allowed to avoid a right or dutiful action; gentleness
can be weakness. "You cannot," she says, "cheat the
dark gods, Mr. Lynch-Gibbon." If he wants his wife
back he has to fight for her. In another discussion,
also with Martin, about Japanese swords, she says the
West associates spirit with softness and with love, the
East, with power, control, discipline.

Martin is both repulsed and deeply attracted to
Honor Klein. Once when he is drunk, he has a sym-

bolic wrestling match with her on a basement floor. Each tries to hurt the other, but there is no crying out on Honor's part, and he follows a kind of Marquis of Queensberry set of rules. At this point we infer that Honor Klein is the Goddess of Reality, Freud's reality principle, and the common man's you-get-what-you-pay-for, and Martin's need to respect himself. Martin is beginning, half in spite of himself, to love her. He follows her back to Cambridge, and goes to her rooms.

Barging into Honor's rooms, he finds her naked and in bed with a man. "She was sitting sideways with the sheet over her legs. Upwards she was as tawny and as naked as a ship's figurehead. I took in her pointed breasts, her black shaggy head of hair, her face stiff and expressionless as carved wood." The man with her is Palmer, her half brother.

At one fell swoop we see the magician of psyches, Palmer, is himself sick and strange, and, apparently, that the Goddess of Reality has feet of clay. Abashed, Martin returns to London, and to Antonia. But she continues self-indulgent, neurotic, and aimless, and he is unhappy with her. Alas, Martin is still in love with Honor Klein. When he confronts her with this knowledge, she tells him he ought to return to his wife—but clearly she is also attracted to him.

Near the end there is a sorting out of couples equal to anything in a Shakespeare comedy. It turns out that Alexander, who is something of a bastard, and Antonia have been having an affair. These two minor characters pair off together—and the reader feels they richly deserve each other. Palmer and Honor appear headed for America together. From a distance, at the airport, Martin sees Palmer and Honor with Georgie, and believes they have somehow enchanted Georgie. Depressed, he returns to his rooms. Shortly, Honor appears, telling him that Palmer and Georgie, who of all the characters has the firmest hold on reality, have gone to America together, and will not return.

Honor, with whom Martin is still in love, says her incestuous relationship is finished. (Perhaps her weakness in this matter is meant to imply that no goddess, and no principle, is wholly reliable.) She remains mysterious, insolent, ironic, and refuses to promise Martin happiness. But she does accept him—because he wants her. It is a strange, grotesque love affair: a man who suddenly, in middle age, wants to be free from the amorality and indulgences with which he had lived for years falls in love with the dark goddess who will exact payment from him for each indulgence, cause him to be constantly alert for his weaknesses, and whose physical unattractiveness will be a continual reminder of things-as-they-are or can be in an often harsh world.

Martin's future is unpredictable, as is the future of any character in a Murdoch novel. But he has chosen to act out of motives that may help him, and will probably save him from his weaker self. Honor Klein would say the future is unknown, but you can put one foot carefully ahead of the other. With luck, this method could take you where you want to go, wherever that may be, and however strange your method of deciding why you wanted to go there in the first place.

It is clear by now that Miss Murdoch is a kind of twentieth-century Congreve. Her characters are interesting puppets and interesting symbols, and she can make them dance or place them erect in an eerie green light. An intellectual game is going on. There is no sweat, no anguish, and no real love making. All of these are illusions. The real game is between Miss Murdoch and her reader, not between the reader and the characters. This is her strength and her limitation.[8]

KINGSLEY AMIS' novel *Lucky Jim* has gone through
more than twenty printings since its publication in
1954. It has also been made into a movie. Jim Dixon,
the hero of *Lucky Jim*, has become a legendary figure.
As J. D. Scott, an English critic, has said, "Angry
Young Men and Lucky Jims have a good deal in common with flying saucers. People disagree violently
about whether they exist. They create passionate confusion. They are potent myths of contemporary society." The chief of the angry young men is John
Osborne, the author of *Look Back in Anger*. Kingsley
Amis does not belong in the same category. He is a
satirist, but not an angry one.

Amis was born in 1922, into a comfortable lower
middle-class London family. His father was a clerk,
and apparently not a bookish man. Amis won a scholarship to a large London day school. ("I'm not the
'beneficiary of Welfare State education' that one or
two writers seem to think I am; I was born too soon.")
It was an excellent school,[1] with a broad cross section
of the social strata. One of his friends was a Jew from
the poor quarter of London's East End, and another
was the son of a prominent church dignitary. He
specialized in classics until he was sixteen, then
switched to English. He attended St. John's, Oxford,

also on a scholarship. He says he liked St. John's because many of the students had backgrounds similar to his and were there because they were good students. In the University at large he found "a good deal of the exclusive spirit" operating.

His university training was interrupted by the Army. He became an officer because of the class system ("I was on the winning side now, because 'an Oxford man' was likely to be enough of a 'gentleman' to do all right as an officer."), and served in the Royal Signals. He was in Normandy in June ("late June, thank God"), 1944. After service in France, Belgium, and West Germany, he was demobilised, in October, 1945. ("If I hadn't been a scholarship-holder it would have been 1946, which shows what an education can do for you!")

Back at Oxford, he worked hard and got a First. He tried but failed to pass a research degree. He wrote a novel and some verse ("none any good"). He married, and took a job at Swansea in 1949, where he remained until a visit to Princeton in 1958–59. He now resides in Oxford, devoting himself to writing.

Amis describes his interests as including television, films, jazz, science fiction (he has written a science fiction play for radio), and the Welsh. He says he has no quarrel with society and recognizes that he has been very fortunate. ("I don't really like being thought of as a 'social novelist.' I have ideas about society, naturally, but human behaviour is what I see myself writing about.")

Although Amis is not, as already noted, to be thought of as belonging in the Angry Young Men category, he has certain connections with the Movement. Some of the poets who appeared in the Movement anthologies Amis knows quite well, others hardly at all. He has been friends with Philip Larkin, John

Wain and Robert Conquest for a long time. He first knew Larkin at St. John's in 1941, as we have seen, and regards him as his best friend. They hold a good many critical tenets in common, though not all ("e.g., he is very pro-D. H. Lawrence, I very anti-"). He sees Larkin's poetry as superior to his own. He and Elizabeth Jennings were also friends at Oxford, but at that time she had not started writing poetry. Enright, he had not met at the time *Poets of the 1950's* was published. Thom Gunn, John Holloway, and Donald Davie he met once at an English teachers' conference.

Amis says he does not admire all of these poets equally, although he believes something good can be said for all of them. All of them desire to write sensibly, "without emotional hoo-ha." They want to be intelligible. He says there may be occasional obscurities in their poems but no riddles. But Amis does not feel that these attitudes make them a "movement." "All the 'movement' thing came from critics and reviewers."

The tone of Amis' autobiographical comments is critical, self-aware, witty, but not cynical. He was quite satisfied with his job at Swansea, and longed neither for a post at Oxford or Cambridge nor for the literary life of London. If he is critical of the caste system it is on legitimate grounds. Whatever quarrels he is likely to have with society are those a reasonable man would want to have. His dislike of such abstractions as "society" may have betrayed him into not recognizing the degree to which he is a social novelist —but this is another matter. He recognizes that in his schooling and his writing career he has been quite fortunate.

Amis' public, as opposed to his critical, reputation may be termed a fluke. It is dependent on Lucky Jim, a type of the educated young man who does not aspire

to be a "gentleman." Because this attitude has become
more and more widespread in England and is perhaps
the beginning of a different sort of cultural allegiance
for the university-educated, Jim has become a myth.
For generations, many people in England have worked
very hard to become gentlemen—then there arises the
phenomenon of a new generation, born into the lower
middle-class or working class, having no such ambition. The culture they are interested in is different
from the traditional "Oxford accented" culture, and
they are even uneasy with the word culture itself. The
relationship of Jim to this realigning of classes and
values is a part of the sociology of the novel. But there
is also the question of Amis' achievements as a literary
man, as critic, poet, and novelist.

## ii

In addition to *New Maps of Hell* (1960), a
study of science fiction, Amis has published well over
one hundred articles and reviews, mostly in the *Spectator*. It is in the *Spectator* pieces that his characteristic manner emerges most clearly, a nimble in-
tellectuality, wit, and a willingess to hit out hard at
pretentiousness in any form. Early short articles and
reviews in *Essays in Criticism* and in *Twentieth Century* show some of these qualities but they are a little
on the academic side, rather quiet and cautious.

Amis is opposed to turning writers into cults,
whether the author is D. H. Lawrence, George Orwell,
or Ivy Compton-Burnett. In his review of Robert Li-
dell's *The Novels of I. Compton-Burnett*,[2] Amis acknowledges the brilliance of Miss Burnett's dialogue
but insists that her inventiveness is often extremely
limited. The situations in her novels commonly involve "infidelity, bastardy, deception and revelation."
Revelations involve hidden letters and eavesdropping.

"There is something almost lazy about this procedure; it exempts the author from having to construct a chain of incidents such as is likely in fact to determine change and progress in human lives, substituting a mere arbitrary framework within the divisions of which no development is called for." He also questions the unreality of some of Miss Burnett's dialogue. But Amis is not trying to demolish her as a novelist —he acknowledges her wonderful comic sense and the depth of her passion, adding that at least two of her novels are masterpieces. His criticism is intended to clarify the nature of Miss Burnett's achievement, whereas cultist criticism merely blurs it.

The majority of Amis' *Spectator* reviews are of the weekly journalism variety, sprightly but not very profound. Some are about books of no real importance. On the other hand, a number of them make his critical preferences very clear. His review of the Penguin *Byron*[3] exhibits his preference for the antiromantic, the air of reality and wit. He disagrees with Mr. Glover, the editor of *Byron*, that Byron's flaw was a lack of metaphysics or mysticism. He says, "Byron is neither narrow nor merely 'light'; his magnificent imaginative sobriety, a gift discovered late and still not perfected when he died, permitted him to tackle a poem appealing to the whole range of human interests. When it is recognized that *Don Juan* is a better poem than the *Prelude*, not only will Byron have attained his true place in English poetry, but English poetry itself—the part of it that is still being written—will have acquired a valuable model." Byron's tone is antiromantic, his subject matter is this world, and his verse is composed of common words in their usual order, a formula very much to Amis' taste. Amis also admires Thomas Love Peacock,[4] and for much the same reasons—he is energetic, original, enchantingly urbane. He places Peacock as a minor master, a writer who commanded "a whole range between witty seriousness and demented knockabout—something which disappeared from the English novel almost before it had properly arrived."

Amis' antiromantic bias comes out more directly in his reviews of Lawrence's *Selected Literary Criticism*,[5] and Dylan Thomas' *A Prospect of the Sea*.[6] Lawrence, he says, was

> one of the great denouncers, the great missionaries the English send to themselves to tell them they are crass, gross, lost, dead, mad and addicted to unnatural vice. I suppose it is a good thing that these chaps continue to roll up, though in this case I wonder whether as much silly conduct has not been encouraged as heartless conduct deterred. However that may be, it is a chilling disappointment to take an actual look at the denunciations and be confronted not only by egomania, fatuity and gimcrack theorising, but bitterness and censoriousness too. It might even be more intelligent to leave Lawrence on his pinnacle, inspiring, unapproachable and unread.

He says that seven-eighths of Lawrence's criticism is valueless, filled with paranoid outbursts, sixth-form smartness, and ignorant dismissals of science and philosophy. Amis' percentage, seven-eighths, is undoubtedly a little high, but considering his position, his preference for sane, rational views of the world, the general evaluation may be right. As E. M. Forster said, the audience for Lawrence is one having a great tolerance for angry prophets.

Amis obviously does not like the bardic types, whether English novelist or Welsh poet. His review of Thomas' *A Prospect of the Sea* (he calls him "Thomas the Rhymer") follows the line one expects. He admires *Portrait of the Artist as a Young Dog* for its humor and its truthfulness. He dislikes what he calls "a sort of verbal free-for-all in which anything whatsoever may or may not be mentioned," and in illustration quotes a wildly fanciful paragraph, full of poles of summer sea-ends, four breasted stems, and other unnatural entities. Amis says that Thomas had genius but wasted it trying to please "those who hanker after something sublimer than thought."

Amis has also written a short piece on the post-war satiric novel, "Laughter To Be Taken Seriously." [7] In it he says the difference between the satire of Dryden, Pope, Butler and Swift and the new satire is that the earlier satire has grandeur and even grandiosity whereas the new satire has humor and realism. The one earlier writer with whom it bears comparison is Fielding. Amis says England's present society is one inviting a golden age of satire:

> New kinds of privilege are in the ascendant, each battling for mastery; at this stage the vices and follies of the social climb and the economic rat-race offer themselves for deflation. Until the new society is simplified and stabilized, which may not be for decades, we are in for what I have called a golden age of satire. It will be inferior in wit and urbanity to the modes which have preceded it, but in humour, vigor and breadth of scope it is likely to prove superior.

He describes the novel as written by Iris Murdoch, John Wain, and presumably himself as a combination of the "violent and the absurd, the grotesque and the romantic, the farcical and the horrific." He does not attempt to say why these particular elements get into the brew.

Amis has also done an "Afterword" for a Signet Classic edition of Samuel Butler's *Erewhon*. As one would expect, he approves of Butler's ironic handling of pretentiousness among scientists, professors, church-men, and ordinary John Does.

As a critic, Amis speaks for common sense. Undoubt-edly there are dangers for the writer, even the literary critic, who chooses always to be on the side of com-mon sense. On the other hand, his criticism has a re-freshing quality. He never hints at truths or profun-dities that will go uninvestigated. He has no truck with the arcana that seem somehow to lie at the center of so many of the more pretentious and ambitious books of modern criticism. He gives reasons for his literary preferences, and he delights in calling things by their simple names. His relaxed manner—he even uses phrases like "the daddy of them all" and "lay us in the aisles"—gives his criticism a humane tone. It is honest, astringent, and intelligent.

### iii

Amis has published two poetry pamphlets and one book, A Case of Samples (1956). The pamphlets are A Frame of Mind (1953) [8] and Poems (1954).[9] A Case of Samples is for the most part a selection from A Frame of Mind and Poems. Amis has made this characterization of his own poetry and that of the other University Wits: "The trouble with the newer poets, including myself, is that they are often lucid and nothing else—except arid and bald, and that, on the other hand, the strict forms seem to give them the idea that they can be sentimental and trite as they please provided they do it in terza rima. But their great defi-ciency is meagerness and triviality of subject matter."

It is true that the range of his subject matter is small, but he is not arid or bald. He works hard at being anti-romantic, hard enough so that one could suspect the romantic exerts a strong pull on him. If there is a char-acteristic situation in his poems it is the building up

of, or pointing to, romantic expectations, then under-
mining them. "Aiming at a Million" will serve as an
example:

> And one sort is always trying
> To be champion darling,
> Bush giant, forest king.
>
> Assorted dryads, gentle,
> Raving or doped, shall straddle
> The god-almighty bole.
>
> It can no more be the biggest
> Than one leaf in a forest
> Can dwarf or dry the rest,
>
> And the biggest beauty
> Is almost ugly,
> Is, or soon will be,
>
> Fleshy or animal,
> Or hard and metal.
> Then should it stay small?
>
> None outgrows dying,
> But height is the end of growing.
> A lot is better than nothing.

"A lot is better than nothing." Amis is not asking that
life or love or joy be seen or experienced only in mini-
mal ways, but he is asking that we recognize human
limitations.

There are no "big" subjects in *A Case of Samples*.
There is wit but, unlike the novels, there is no farce or
horse-play; altogether, the tone is more subdued. The
subject matter includes sex, love, boredom, various
situations realistically and satirically viewed, and topics of special interest to a lecturer in English literature.

"A Song of Experience," for example, is a witty account of the sex life of a "dark-eyed traveller" who did what "Blake presaged," what "Lawrence took a stand on" and "what Yeats locked up in fable." "Bed and Breakfast," the most clearly romantic poem, is about a man's desire not to have the objects of his sentiments and affection touched by an outsider. "The Real Earth" and "The Silent Room" are realistic views of death; the former is about a woman who was so preoccupied with domesticity that she was caught unaware by death, and the latter contrasts the dreams of immortality with the decay of the body. "Beowulf," "Lessons" and "Masters" are the poems of a scholar and teacher. "A Note on Wyatt" shows clearly how Amis can take an earlier poet's symbol or line and turn it into something very much his own:

> See her come bearing down, a tidy craft!
> Gaily her topsails bulge, her sidelights burn!
> There's jigging in her rigging fore and aft,
> And beauty's self, not name, limned on her stern.
>
> See at her head the Jolly Roger flutters!
> "God, is she fully manned? If she's one short . . ."
> Cadet, bargee, longshoreman, shellback mutters;
> Drowned is reason that should me comfort.
>
> But habit, like a cork, rides the dark flood,
> And, like a cork, keeps her in walls of glass;
> Faint legacies of brine tingle my blood,
> The tide-winds fading echoes, as I pass.
>
> Now, jolly ship, sign on a jolly crew:
> God bless you, dear, and all who sail in you.

One senses an extensive knowledge of literary traditions in this and many other poems. Oddly enough, "A Note on Wyatt" seems to echo Herrick, even though it is also decidedly twentieth-century. Certain poems seem to echo Auden. Several deliberately bait the romantic poetry of the 1940's. No particular eighteenth-century poet seems present as a direct influence, but one is not surprised to learn that Amis' field of specialization is eighteenth-century literature. He is witty, common-sensical, neither cynical nor sentimental, and he writes lucidly.

D. J. Enright says of his and Amis' group that "there is undoubtedly a new spirit stirring in contemporary English poetry, and before long we should be able to define that spirit more accurately and in greater detail." Amis' achievement as a poet is nowhere near that of Eliot or Auden or Thomas, but he has a manner decidedly his own, he has written a number of fine poems, and there is certainly a possibility that his eventual achievement may be a kind of challenge to one or more of them.

### iv

The *Times Literary Supplement* reviewer said Jim Dixon is that "rare thing, an amiable cynic." This is not so. Jim is torn between self-interest and inability to suffer phoney-ness and pretentiousness. He is ingenuous and boy-like in his outrageous conduct and in his hope that luck will serve him. *Lucky Jim* is a curious mixture of realism and fairy tale.

The plot is a simple one, built along Horatio Alger lines, with the difference that Jim does not get to the top through industriousness but through luck. He is a lecturer in history at a provincial university. His specialty is the Middle Ages, a period he dislikes; he had specialized in it because doing so seemed the easiest way of earning a degree. He believes that history could be taught to good purpose but misguided notions and pretentiousness (which he does nothing to rectify) prevent that. His anxieties and ineptness cause him to make a bad initial impression on administration officials, and both his temperament and events conspire to bring his academic career to a disastrous end. Margaret, a neurotic colleague, attaches herself to him, and his effort to break off with her causes, or he thinks could cause, Professor Welch, his immediate superior, to be unsympathetic with him. Welch, a well-intentioned but preposterously bumbling man, bores Jim stiff. Invited to the Welches for a weekend, he gets drunk and burns both his bedclothes and a night table. The Welches learn that he had arranged to be called away Sunday morning—because he could not suffer a whole weekend as their guest. Jim gets into open conflict with the Welches' obnoxious son, Bertrand, over Christine, the girl Bertrand expects at his own convenience to marry. Eventually Jim and Bertrand have a fist fight. The climax of a chain of bad luck is Jim's public lecture on Merrie England. He fortifies himself by drinking sherry and whiskey—and when he stands up to speak he finds himself parodying the delivery of Welch and the Principal and generally ridiculing his subject matter and others like it. Most of the audience, townspeople and his colleagues, are shocked; a few recognize that he had been driven, even against his self-interest, to attack pomposity and pretentiousness. Among the latter is the wealthy Gore-Urquhart, Christine's uncle. When Jim is sacked, Gore-Urquhart offers him the sinecure Bertrand had been seeking. Christine chooses Jim in preference to Bertrand. And off the two of them go, to money and happiness in London. The frontispiece carries this:

> *Oh, lucky Jim,*
> *How I envy him.*
> *Oh, lucky Jim,*
> *How I envy him.*
>                              Old Song

Obviously the plot, assuming it can be abstracted, cannot alone account for the interest one feels in *Lucky Jim*. *Lucky Jim* has other virtues: the characterizations are extremely good, the dialogue is natural, the narrative pacing is excellent, and Jim himself is not only a wonderfully funny character, he is almost archetypal.

Professor Welch, for example, bumbles along, whether talking, driving a car, or directing four-part singing. In the following passage he and Jim are talking about Margaret's recovery from what they believe was an attempted suicide:

> Dixon knew all this, and very much better than Welch could hope to, but he felt constrained to say: "Yes, I see. I think living with you, Professor and Mrs. Welch, must have helped her a lot to get out of the wood."
>
> "Yes, I think there must be something about the atmosphere of the place, you know, that has some sort of healing effect. We had a friend of Peter Warlock's down once, one Christmas it was, years ago it must be now. He said very much the same thing. I can remember myself last summer, coming back from the examiner's conference in Durham. It was a real scorcher of a day, and the train was . . . well, it . . . ."

Coherence is beyond the poor professor. Margaret, the neurotic lecturer, likes emotional scenes. A part of this is what Jim calls her liking for "avowals." On one occasion she and Jim are standing at a pub bar—

> At his side, Margaret heaved a sigh which invariably preluded the worst avowals. She waited until he had to look at her and said: "How close we seem to be tonight, James." A fat-faced man on the other side of her turned and stared at her. "All the barriers down, aren't they?" she asked.
>
> Finding this unanswerable, Dixon gazed at her, slowly nodding his head, half-expecting a round of applause from some invisible auditorium. What wouldn't

he give for a fierce purging draught of fury or contempt, a really efficient worming from the sense of responsibility?

At last she lowered her eyes and might have fallen to scanning her beer for foreign matter. "It seemed almost too much to hope for." After another silence, she went on in a brisker tone. "But can't we sit somewhere more . . . out of the public eye?"

Bertrand pretends to himself and others that he is a good painter, and he uses his role as sensitive artist to bully Christine and others into doing his bidding. Nor is he above using his father's position to threaten Jim. There is nothing subtle or indirect about Bertrand. For example, there is this scene leading to the fist fight:

[Bertrand] seemed in a controlled rage, and was breathing heavily, though this might well have been the result of running up two flights of stairs.

Dixon jumped lightly down to the floor [he had been doing his ape act on his bed when Bertrand entered]; he, too, was panting a little. "What do you want to say?"

"Just this. The last time I saw you, I told you to stay away from Christine. I now discover you haven't done so. What have you got to say about that, to begin with."

The minor characters also have individuality: Michie, the mustached eager student, Caton, the unscrupulous editor, Mrs. Welch, humorless and pushing for her son, Christine, physically attractive but unsure of herself, Carol Goldsmith, frankly in pursuit of sexual pleasure, Catchpole, untidy but will intentioned and concerned to be well thought of, Johns, a toady, and Atkinson, brusque and rather cruel. Most of them appear briefly, and it is a mark of Amis' skill that they emerge clearly. But it is the characterization of Jim himself that lifts *Lucky Jim* above the level of other competently written novels.

During his visit to the Welches, Jim admires their cat, Id. "Dixon bent and tickled Id under the ear. He admired it for never allowing either of the senior Welches to pick it up. 'Scratch 'em,' he whispered to it; 'pee on the carpets.' It began to purr loudly." There is a great deal of Id in Jim which his self-conscious self finds difficult to hold in check. He talks to himself, and loves dirty words and says them to himself on polite and solemn occasions.

One of his devices for releasing emotion is his famous "faces." When Christine, referring to Jim's having left the Welch party to go to a pub, says in a flat, humorless way that he should apologize, Jim turns away and makes "his Chinese mandarin's face, hunching his shoulders a little." Another time, upon hearing Welch's name being paged, Jim huddles deep in his chair "and unobtrusively made his Martian-invader face." Among the faces are his "Eskimo face," his "Evelyn Waugh face," his "Edith Sitwell face," his "shot-in-the-back face," and his "crazy peasant face." When he learns he has won Christine he makes a "sex life in Ancient Rome face." Like his ape imitations, the faces are comic masks. They are expressions of Jim's incredulity, amazement, his clownish interpretations of or reactions to something said or done. Jim is also a fine mimic, and the mimicry too is a means of commenting on pomposity, eccentricity or strangeness.

Jim has been called an anti-hero—and he is. He has more weaknesses than are necesary to make him "human." He is himself on-the-make, even though his fundamental honesty as well as his good luck save him. He is a great exaggerator. He is unnecessarily hard on Welch, who, despite his fuzziness, is well intentioned, and Jim runs from boredom as though it would cause him to sicken and die. His evaluations of people tend to be acidulous. His redeeming feature, of course, is his basic honesty.

At one point, Margaret calls Jim "a shabby little provincial." Insofar as this is true it is in the sense of his being an outsider. As an outsider, he sees through the cultural affectation of the Welches, and he has a sharp eye for what is pretentious in academic life. We are never introduced to Jim's home or family—so there is no way of telling what alternative system, if any, has developed his satirical bent. He seems to carry no traditional views with him. He is on the loose, and it is the academic community that he happens to find himself wandering about in. There is a sense, however, in which Jim trails a child's world after him into his professional life.

In fact the world Jim lives in is in part a child's world. He sees characteristics in caricature. He can be anxiety-ridden or completely irresponsible. Gore-Urquhart turns out to be a good Wizard. He oversees the action and brings it to a successful conclusion, choosing to make Jim a kind of sweepstakes winner. If Jim can be called an archetypal character it is because he typifies a universal desire for good luck, to win the right girl and get all the money one needs. Experience may go against it, but there his success is, romantically there.[10]

*That Uncertain Feeling* (1955), which was also made into a successful movie, is in some ways similar to *Lucky Jim*. John Lewis is the center of the action. Like Jim Dixon he hates dishonesty even though he is sometimes dishonest himself, and he has similar talent for satire. One fairly essential difference is whereas Jim Dixon courts luck, John Lewis tries to steer his own course. A summary of the plot will help.

John Lewis, his wife Jean, and their two children

live in an unattractive second floor apartment in Aberdarcy, Wales. Lewis and Jean were raised in the lower
middle class but are university educated. He has a job
in the local library. Elizabeth Gruffydd-Williams, a
member of the monied community, "Aberdarcy bourgeoisie," takes a fancy to Lewis, and eventually they
"do it." Jean recognizes the situation and tells him that
hereafter they are married in name only. Through
Elizabeth's intervention with her husband Vernon the
sub-librarianship, a substantially better job, is offered
to Lewis. He declines it, resigns from the library, and
moves his family to the town Fforestfawr, where he
and Jean had grown up; he takes a job in the office of
a coal company. Flight from Aberdarcy seemed to him
the only way of saving their marriage. The almost final
scene of the novel is at a party in Fforestfawr. A young
matron, a professor's wife, makes the same sort of ad-
vances to him that Elizabeth had, and he takes off
down the stairs to the street, his wife in sympathetic
pursuit.

There is a good deal of class animus in *That Uncertain Feeling*. Elizabeth Gruffydd-Williams' set are
"Anglicised Welsh," and Lewis dislikes their pretentions. However, he dislikes even more the professional
Welshman and his "Celtic mist." As a kind of intruder
into the Anglicised Welsh set, Lewis readily sees everything, and there is a good deal, that is meretricious.
The taking of the job in Fforestfawr might be looked
upon as a retreat into the lower class as well as a flight
from temptation—the novel ends with a glimpse of
colliers going toward the pub. "At the pub door we
had to wait for a moment until the way cleared ahead
of us. To anyone watching it might have looked as if
Jean and I, too, were coming off shift." There is some
nostalgia and affection here, and perhaps the suggestion that Lewis and his wife are trying to re-enter the

world of their childhoods. It should be pointed out too that Lewis' father is an upright character whose watch-words are "sobriety and decorum." The collective virtue of the lower class however is not investigated, and anyhow Amis is too sophisticated to set up one class as morally superior to another. Presumably, we are to see Lewis as a man with both a "generalised lust" and a "conscience." There are also references to his "rootless apprehension, indefinite restlessness, and in-activating boredom," but he does not appear to be overwhelmed by his library position or by the "Aber-darcy bourgeoisie." His milieu happens to have been a double world, the one opened to him through his uni-versity education and the one he had known as a child. The social worlds that Lewis inhabits do not bear significantly on his "problem." It may not be unfair to say the novel breaks in two, one half being con-cerned with Lewis' "problem," the other half with his characterizations of the people he lives with.

Amis can apparently create a striking comic type at will. For example, there is Mrs. Davies, the tired and humorless crone who lives in the flat below the Lewises. On one occasion when Jean is out and he is baby-sitting, Lewis has the following encounter:

"Mr. Lewis. Are you there, Mr. Lewis?" I went out to the landing. "Is there someone calling?" I asked in my special cultured accent, which I retained for the whole of the subsequent dialogue.

"Is that you, Mr. Lewis?"

"That's Mrs. Davies, isn't it? Well, and how are you, Mrs. Davies? Long time no see, as they say."

"Your baby's crying, Mr. Lewis. Crying a long time, she've been, poor little soul."

"I think you must be making a mistake, Mrs. Davies: our baby's a little boy. And he's fast asleep now, you know."

"The little girl crying then, is it? Don't make no difference, do it, Mr. Lewis?"

I could see her in the gloom of the passage, bent forward with her arms across her waist.

Lewis regularly carries on this kind of subdued warfare with Mrs. Davies. His relationships with others, whether affectionate, sympathetic, proper, or impersonal are also rendered effectively. Very clearly one sees Jean, Mr. and Mrs. Jenkins, Elizabeth and Vernon Gruffydd-Williams, the dentist and his mistress, Gareth Probert the poet, and the officials who interview the candidates for the sub-librarian post. Amis' inclination is to treat his characters satirically, and almost the only ones who escape this are Jean and Vernon Gruffydd-Williams.

Lewis has a down-to-earth, rather unimaginative, approach to culture. While awaiting his interview he imagines the board asking, "Are you interested in films, drinking, women's breasts, American novels, jazz, science fiction?" Lewis is interested in one and all of the items. But he can spot affectation in any of its manifestations, an "elocutionist" pronunciation of a word as well as the pervasive dishonesty of Probert's Welsh "culture," in *The Martyr*. Probert's drama, incidentally, allows Amis to attack the "mushy manner of the forties," with a side-swipe at T. S. Eliot. These lines open the chapter devoted to the play:

"When in Time's double morning, meaning death,
Denial's four-eyed bird, the Petrine cock,
Crew junction down the sleepers of the breath,
Iron bled that dry tree at the place of rock,
The son of dog snarled at the rat of love,
Holy-in-corner of the tottered sky,
Where angel tiered on angle swung above,
Into each crack and crick and creek of eye,
Angels on horseback wept with vinegar. . . ."

This is Lewis' explication:

> A few moments of whimsical prose at the beginning had hinted that the protagonist, The Martyr himself, had done something, that other people intended to do something to him because of what he'd done, and that The Monk didn't want them to do it. Apart from this there were various linguistic clues, and I felt myself on safe ground in inferring that the whole business was rather on the symbolical side. Words like "death" and "life" and "man" cropped up every few lines, but were never attached to anything concrete or specific. "Death," for example, wasn't my death or your death or his death or her death or our death or their death or my Aunt Fanny's death, but just death, and in the same way "love" wasn't my, etc.,

With a few changes, this could be a passage in one of Amis' critical pieces.

In *That Uncertain Feeling*, Amis is more persistently or at least more obviously in search of a theme then he is in *Lucky Jim*. It is not a very profound theme. As we have already seen, Amis' gifts as a novelist are considerable. He invents easily, creating situations and planting characters wherever they are needed to move the action along. And he has a wonderful sense of farce. The scene, for example, in which he escapes from the Gruffydd-Williams' house by posing as a plumber and then donning a woman's dress and hat is like something out of *Charley's Aunt* or a 1920's movie. It is so extremely funny in itself that only after finishing the book does one realize that the episode is not quite in keeping with Lewis' character or with other episodes in the book. Amis' gifts seem sometimes almost to run away with him.

*I Like It Here* (1958), Amis' third novel, is disappointing. It is amusing enough as a little adventure story told by a satiric minded narrator, but it must be

generally disappointing to those readers who felt that
*Lucky Jim* and *That Uncertain Feeling* represented a
new development in English fiction. One of Amis'
problems apparently is that he has not known whether
he was writing farce or social satire, or, better, what
degree of farce he could allow into the social satire
without turning the latter into farce. *I Like It Here*
avoids the dilemma by getting outside English society
almost altogether and getting a down-to-earth, no-
nonsense view of a holiday in Portugal; the adventure
story is tacked on to add a little suspense.

The central character, Garnet Bowen, is Jim Dixon
and John Lewis over again. The family situation is
similar to that in *That Uncertain Feeling*—only this
time the wife is Barbara and there are three rather than
two children. Their original home is Swansea but they
now live in London. All this is remarkably close to
Amis' own family situation. And Amis' failure to provide a new set of basic characters is also disappointing.

Garnet Bowen won a First at Swansea, worked on
papers, at first in Swansea and later in London, and is
now free-lancing. He has one book behind him—"a
collection of tarted-up reviews called *No Dogmas*."
Behind the Portugal trip is an invitation to write an
article for the American magazine *SEE* and to check
on the very popular novelist Wulfstan Strether.
Strether, who lives in Portugal, had kept his identity a
secret from all but one member (now dead) of his
publishing firm. He had announced ten years earlier
that he had finished writing, but now he has sent in a
new manuscript, and added he intends to come to
London to receive the acclaim he knows awaits him
there. The publishers feel that they may be dealing
with an impostor and want Bowen to find out the
facts.

Insofar as the novel has a theme, it is that England

is a fine, comfortable place, and that foreigners, looked
at through English eyes, are even queerer than the
English. There are little jibes at French lucidity
("their high regard for Poe, for Charles Morgan. God,
yes"), at the high-handedness of the Portuguese government, and so on. The title, *I Like It Here*, means
Garnet Bowen is pleased to live in London. Amis does
not seem much engaged by his theme—he merely uses
it to hang a story on.

Wulfstan Strether turns out to be a rather nice but
ingenuous old gent, convinced that he is the greatest
writer of the twentieth century. Amis maintains suspense about Bowen's mission by withholding positive
identification of Strether until the final pages. A good
many Amis types—Mrs. Knowles, Bowen's mother-in-
law, Oates, the eccentric Englishman, Harry Bannion,
who does burlesque renditions of Victorian poems,
Dr. Lopez, a possible extortionist, Emilia, Lopez's attractive friend, and many others—move in procession
under Bowen's satiric eyes. But the characterizations
are less vigorously done than in the two earlier novels.
And Garnet Bowen himself is less vigorous than Jim
Dixon or John Lewis.

*That Uncertain Feeling* and *I Like It Here* have
commonly been seen as lesser novels than *Lucky Jim*,
even as a decided falling off from a most promising
beginning. *Take a Girl Like You* (1960) is not so good
as *Lucky Jim*, but it is better than the other two, and
may bode well for Amis' future as a novelist.

Amis is trying to enlarge his subject. There are
signs of growth and development, as well as indica-
tions that he is still looking over his shoulder at some
of his earlier successes. Patrick Standish is not unlike
Jim Dixon. Both are quick with words, and always
capable of coming up with an appropriate wisecrack.
A school secretary named Charlton gives promise of

being another Bertrand Welch. He is quite as obnoxious, and is a tempting target for Patrick's barbs. But
Amis resists the temptation to duplicate earlier scenes,
and Charlton all but drops from the action. Jenny
Bunn, Amis' most highly developed female character,
is pretty and desirable, but Amis tries to keep her in
the normal girl category. It would have been easy to
make her "dumb" or "way out." He seems deliberately
to be avoiding either slapstick or the bizarre.

*A Girl Like You* dramatizes a contest between
Jenny, a schoolmistress, whose appearance raises eye-
brows, male and female, and Patrick, who teaches
Latin. The contest is for her "virtue." The contest is
not in the manner of Restoration comedy, in which
each act promises an offstage bedroom situation. The
background of the novel is dreary. The characters are
Welfare State, declassed, humdrum. Lechery, for
many of them, is a relatively inexpensive way of putting a little excitement into their lives.

Jenny and Patrick belong to this new English society. She has her rented room, run by an unambitious
landlord, David Thompson, and his justifiably suspicious and jealous wife. Another roomer, Anna le Page,
is an arty lesbian, and she pretends to be French.
Patrick has his small bachelor quarters, a lair for seduc-
tions. They visit "classy" restaurants, road houses,
pubs, listen to jazz. Patrick's soft speeches, outrage-
ously exaggerating Jenny's charms, are invariably made
in a boozy atmosphere. No one is very sure about the
rules for sexual morality. Not even Jenny. But she has
had a strict upbringing, and she trusts her instinct.

Unintentionally and unwittingly Patrick falls in love
with Jenny. He continues to try to seduce her. During
a long drunken party, near the end of the book, Jenny,
in self-protection, goes to bed, Patrick follows, and she
is too drunk to resist him. Patrick has mixed feelings

about his victory. He is glad that the struggle is over. He knows he loves her. And he feels deeply ashamed of himself. Jenny too has mixed feelings. She is angry that Patrick has taken advantage of her drunkenness, and says she is through with him. Yet she is rather relieved she is no longer a virgin. And she knows she loves him.

*Take a Girl Like You* is far from being a great novel. But it is not a dull one. There is excitement in watching a talented writer investigate a new and interesting subject. Amis is able to present the manners and morals of a changing society. In *Take a Girl Like You*, he is dealing with a society that has not discovered a new system of status to replace an older and undoubtedly partly unjust system. Amis is not attacking the Establishment, at least not here; it is hardly in evidence in this novel. He is dealing with the curious and perhaps unexpected ways in which conduct and morality are related to status. It is a new subject, and the occasion of his insights and the source of his comedy.

### v

Amis' Fabian pamphlet *Socialism and the Intellectuals* (1957), published by the Fabian society, is an attempt to account for his attitudes toward the Labour Party, to account for his apathy toward that party and toward politics generally. Essentially the pamphlet says that intellectuals by and large do not know very much about politics, are too concerned with general principles, and rightly do not carry much weight in politics. He thinks that self-interest is the motivating force in politics and that it is right that this be so. It is understandable that *Socialism and the Intellectuals* roused a furor in liberal journals, most of which found it an abdication from responsibility. Almost anyone with liberal principles could make out a

pretty strong case against it. It is however a good introduction to the state of mind that Amis has called "that
uncertain feeling." Perhaps the key point is Amis'
claim that the intellectual belongs to no social group
and is therefore restless and uneasy.

The Welfare State, Amis says, has elevated the economic level of the average worker to a level equal to or
above that of the average intellectual. "The Welfare
State, indeed, is notoriously unpopular with intellectuals. It was all very well to press for higher working
class wages in the old days, but now that all wages
have risen the picture is less attractive; why, some of
them are actually better off than we are ourselves. We
never contemplated *that*." They will acknowledge
that the Welfare State helped make their academic
and literary careers possible, but this does not make
them feel any urgent sense of gratitude. The intellectual, he says, in comparison with the steelworker or
the banker has no political interests to defend except
the very general one of not getting himself bossed
around by a totalitarian government.

The attention given to *Socialism and the Intellectuals*, like the attention given to *Lucky Jim*, suggests
that Amis is looked to as a voice, perhaps the chief
voice, of his generation, or at least of his group. Stephen Spender says that just as Auden was the acknowl-
edged leader of his generation, so Kingsley Amis is of
his. Amis, however, is not a forthright deliverer of manifestoes, and does not desire to court other writers as
followers. When asked to contribute to *Declaration*,[11]
a book of manifestoes, he declined, saying, "I hate all
this pharisaical twittering about the 'state of our civilization' and I suspect anyone who wants to buttonhole
me about my 'role in society.' This book is likely to
prove a valuable addition to the cult of the Solemn
Young Man; I predict a great success for it." Amis has

also been very explicit, as in his comments on Lawrence, in criticizing the cult of leadership.

In another place, he has said the novelist should avoid whatever might turn him away from being a novelist. The novelist ought not to take a stand on "his predicament as a Western intellectual," he should "avoid generalizing about contemporary culture, the position of the artists, etc. Otherwise he may find himself turning into a publicist." Nor does he see much point in the lumping of his novels with those of John Wain and Iris Murdoch. He is not eager to be thought of as a part of a school of novelists. (He is, of course, aware of the publicity value that talk of a school makes possible.) "It is very difficult," he says, "for a writer who is told he is part of a school to prevent himself from either trying to write as the school is supposed to write, or else breaking his neck to prove he is different."

Despite his unwillingness to assume the role of leader or voice of the 1950's, perhaps Amis is to be so viewed. His reviews and essays provide a pretty coherent statement of a critical position, and his poetry and fiction provide models for writers who may wish to imitate him. And there is *Socialism and the Intellectuals* for those who might want to know what one should feel about intellectuals in the Welfare State.

As a critic, Amis has helped to formulate a set of conventions and points of view that are agreeable to his generation. As poet, he has exhibited many of the virtues and undoubtedly some of the limitations of these conventions. Any fair-minded reader will allow a group of writers their critical principles and their conventions. The important thing is the level of achievement they help make possible. Amis' criticism is largely directed against sham, and he is critical of various kinds of verbal and structural imprecision. It is a valuable sort of criticism. It is too early to tell what its total influence will be. His poetry is interesting but considerably less distinguished than that of some of his eminent elders.

Amis' fiction is without question something different in that it not only questions the position of the English gentleman, but shows the beginnings of a different sort of culture. The pre-Amis novel usually respected the gentleman's code, his privileges and his pursuits. Samuel Butler said, "All nature strains and groans to produce an English 'swell.'" In Amis' novels nature, or whatever, strains and groans but not to the end of producing the gentleman and the gentleman's world. But, as Amis says, Jim Dixon, if pressed, would admit that culture is important and ought to be available to everyone regardless of his social origins or school connections. Despite his dislike of being thought of as a social novelist, Amis' novels are social documents.

*Lucky Jim, That Uncertain Feeling,* and *I Like It Here* are very well executed, and of course they are very funny. They do not however have at their center any very profound searching out of psychological or philosophical principles. Nor do they really take a stand on the social conflict between classes. Another way of putting this is to say that the novels seem not to evolve or grow from a premise or a thesis. Amis has a great flair for the zany and the outrageous. There is social satire too, much of it brilliantly done. Even so, one feels that something is missing. What Amis actually does in these novels is to take off the affectations of the genteel and the pretentious. But it is not enough that Jim Dixon and John Lewis and Garnet Bowen burlesque the university world, the small town "bourgeoisie," or travel snobs. These novels imply alternative values, and it is these that are insufficiently explored. In *A Girl Like You* Amis has addressed himself to the relationship of moral decisions to the factor of status. This is a subject that has long engaged novelists, and since he has chosen to examine it one could say there is a good possibility that Amis has an important career ahead of him.

# 6 THE OTHER WRITERS:
## A COMMON VIEW

THE OTHER WRITERS in this group, Robert Conquest, Dennis Enright, John Holloway, Donald Davie, Elizabeth Jennings, and Thom Gunn, have received less acclaim than Larkin, Wain, Amis and Miss Murdoch. They are not without interest. Broadly speaking, their writings reflect a new social order in England, and imply that the period of Modernism, as associated with the work of Yeats, Joyce, Lawrence, Eliot, Auden and Dylan Thomas, is over.

Traditionally, England has had a "gentleman" culture. Education in the public schools and at Oxford and Cambridge was for the gentleman. Gifted young men from the lower classes who pushed their way upward attempted and sometimes succeeded in taking on the accent and the points of view of the gentleman. After World War II, with the multiplication of scholarships of various sorts, the gentleman's domination of English culture began to wane.

Simultaneously there was a reaction against the writers who had dominated English literature between World War I and World War II. The intensities of modern criticism, and the experiments that had been carried out in poetry and fiction seem suddenly to have come to an end. Different critical values have replaced the old ones, and different conventions replaced those that had dominated poetry and fiction for about thirty years. The evidence for this is in the criticism, poetry, and fiction of Conquest, Enright, and the others.

### ii

Robert Conquest's family background is quite different from that of most of the other Movement poets, and he is the only one who has not had a professional university connection. He was born in 1917 in Malvern. His father's family, Virginian in origin, settled in England near the turn of the century. His mother's family "are generals, admirals, Indian governors and barristers and so on." Conquest was in part raised on the Riviera, and went to "socially top schools"—then to Magdalen College, Oxford, and to the University of Grenoble. During the War he served in the Oxford and Bucks Light Infantry, in Italy and the Balkans. Since the War he has worked for the Foreign Office, in Sofia, New York and London. In the spring of 1962 Lippincott published his *Pasternak Affair*, a study of censorship and intimidation in Russia. He believes his relationship with other Movement poets is a matter of temperament, not of class. The temperamental similarities he defines as "anti-phoney" and "anti-wet." These poets, he says, refuse to be intimidated by any set of theoreticians, whether literary or political.

Conquest's poems have been appearing in literary periodicals since about 1940. In 1945, he was awarded the Brazil Prize for a long poem, and in 1951 he was a prize-winner in the Festival of Britain poetry competition. In 1953, he was a co-editor of *New Poems*, a P.E.N. Anthology. His friendship with Movement poets began about 1952. Between 1953–56, he had a small house in Hampstead—"with room to put people up." He says: "Amis and his wife, Enright and his wife and daughter, Davie, Wain and Larkin stayed with me for an odd night or nights when they came to London—the Amises quite frequently."

Conquest says he accepted the invitation of Macmillan to edit *New Lines* because too many editors of literary magazines had not got around to publishing the sort of poetry he admired. The introduction, he says, was pitched at a rather "low and general level, both to reach and to stir up a bit, a fair-sized audience, which on the whole it did." These paragraphs pretty much catch what he was trying to achieve as editor of *New Lines*:

> If one had briefly to distinguish this poetry of the fifties from its predecessors, I believe the most important general point would be that it submits to no great systems of theoretical constructs nor agglomerations of unconscious commands. It is free from both mystical and logical compulsions and—like modern philosophy —is empirical in its attitude to all that comes. This reverence for the real person or event is, indeed, a part of the general intellectual ambience (in so far as that is not blind or retrogressive) of our time. One might, without stretching matters too far, say that George Orwell with his principle of real, rather than ideological, honesty, exerted, even though indirectly, one of the major influences on modern poetry.
>
> On the more technical side, though of course related to all this, we see refusal to abandon a rational structure and comprehensible language, even when the verse is most highly charged with sensuous or emotional intent.

Conquest's evaluations of *New Lines* poets are that Larkin "is a very fine poet, that Amis, at his best, is admirably ebullient and effective, but on the whole that Thom Gunn seems to be (at least potentially) the most remarkable of the lot." None of the *New Lines* poets, he says, writes long poems or even a great many short poems. The reason, he thinks, is that all of them have jobs requiring hard work and leaving them little time for poetry.

Several of the New University Wits have said they wanted no more poems about other poems, about works of art, or foreign cities—that this sort of thing seemed like name-dropping, showing that one knew the right people. Conquest, on the contrary, writes about the classical poets, Hart Crane, Stendhal, foreign cities, and the theory of art. There is throughout his *Poems* [1] the suggestion of a sensitive cosmopolitan mind searching out a sense of order, and asking, over and over, how the poet contributes to order. "Poetry in 1944" says explicitly that his poetry is a search for order:

> . . . *For I must believe*
> *That somewhere the poet is working who can handle*
> *The flung world and his own heart. To him I say*
> *The little I can. I offer him the debris*
> *Of five years' undirected storm in self and Europe,*
> *And my love. Let him take it for what it's worth.*
> *And this poem scarcely made and already forgotten.*

Apparently Conquest sees the poet as one searching for a balance between the Apollonian and Dionysian, as well as bringing or trying to bring his personal hopes and aspirations into a viable relationship with the external world. One of his most interesting expressions of these themes is in his poem about an eventual landing on Mars, "The Landing in Deucalion":

> *Screened by the next few decades from our vision*
> *Their image, none the less, is fairly clear,*
> *Emerging from the air-lock into light*
> *Sharp, unfamiliar in its composition,*
> *From cold stars and a small blue flaming sun*
> *As glints of racing Phobos disappear.*

*Leaving the rocket pointing at that sky*
*Their steps and sight turn to the chosen spot*
*Through this thin air through which the thin winds keen;*
*The valves hiss in their helmets as they cross*
*The crumbling sand towards the belt of green*
*Where long-sought strangeness will reveal—what?*

*And why this subject should be set to verse*
*Is only partly in what fuels their hearts*
*More powerful than those great atomic drives*
*(Resembling as it does the thrust of poetry—*
*The full momentum of the poets' whole lives)*
*—Its consummation is yet more like art's:*

*For as they reach that unknown vegetation*
*Their thirst is given satisfaction greater*
*Than ever found but when great art results;*
*Not just new detail or a changed equation*
*But freshly flaming into all the senses*
*And from the full field of the whole gestalt.*

*And so I sing them now, as others later.*

These themes are persistent, in poem after poem.

What is rather disturbing about Conquest's poems
is that they open or raise questions but rarely resolve
them. Perhaps this is inevitably penalty for the contemporary poet who writes about aesthetic and philosophical questions, except for those major poets who
are able to create a coherent vision of man as a thinking, imagining and believing creature. Only Eliot,
Yeats, and Stevens in our time have made the necessary effort, and not even they wholly succeeded. Next
to their work however, Conquest's poems look very
tentative. But it is to his credit that he essays questions that only major talents can resolve with some degree of forthrightness.

One of Conquest's interests is science fiction, an

interest he shares with Amis. Together, as we have
seen, they edited an anthology of science fiction. Both
of them believe science fiction offers challenges to the
imagination and serious opportunities for the novelist.
He has written a number of science-fiction book reviews for *The Spectator*. In his own science-fiction
novel, *A World of Difference* (1955) [2] he is concerned
with the effects on human beings of continuous social
and technological changes.

*A World of Difference* is not a good novel. Even so,
it can be read with some interest. The year is 2007,
and a revolution against the state is under way. The
state is a modified form of Western democracy. The
revolutionists, for the most part, are of the Stalinist
variety, given to taking deviationists off to the nearest
wall or into a tunnel (a lot of the action, especially
on other planets, is underground—because of the ab-
sence of oxygen or because the atmosphere is radioactive) to be shot. Possibly because of the need to
explain or to concentrate on twenty-first century gad-
getry, characterization is minimized. Therefore it is
sometimes hard to remember who is speaking or being
discussed. And the story line is sometimes lost sight of.

In *A World of Difference*, man moves with tremen-
dous speed over the surface of the earth and out into
space, to Pluto, Mars, the Moon, and to space stations.
But human beings are still human beings—there are
phonies, hacks, true artists, girls with attractive per-
sonalities, men who are serious students, or thugs, or
bad jet drivers. Man learns to adjust to continuous
change, and hopes he will not destroy himself.

Conquest makes a few references to the present
world, to the old London (it is radioactive), and even
to the poetry quarrels of the 1940's and 1950's. Cruis-
ers that fight for the government in the revolution are
named the *Amis*, the *Gunn*, the *Holloway*, the *Wain*,

the *Enright*, the *Larkin*, and the *Jennings*. There is no explanation of the names—but presumably the brave new world of 2007 is memorializing a brave little band of the 1950's.

### iii

Dennis Enright (he sometimes signs himself D. J. Enright) was born in Leamington in 1920, into a working-class family. His father, a postman, was a Dubliner in exile; he died in 1934. His mother was an ex-domestic. After elementary school, he won a scholarship to Leamington College. Having done very well on the School Certificate he went on another scholarship to Downing College, where F. R. Leavis was his tutor.

In *Heaven Knows Where*, his second novel, Enright has Packet (who seems to be his fictional alter ego) say this of the second section of *The Waste Land*, where the scene shifts to one of low life:

> It recites well, like real music hall stuff. But unhappily for me the poet is talking about the kind of people among whom I was born and brought up. Lil, Albert, Bill, Lou, and May—for me they possess neither the glamour of squalor nor the aura of rumbustiousness. As I remember them (and mind you, I should be quite ready to forget them, if I could), they were neither ill-conditioned beasts nor earthbound gods. They did the things which you expected—like having their teeth out, and wanting a good time—and then they did things which you didn't expect. So you looked silly—as you always do when you generalize.

Throughout his books, Enright takes an unsentimental view of class. He also casts a rather cold eye on anything that is pretentious or arty, which could be an attitude he owes to his social origins.

Enright's review of Richard Hoggart's *The Uses of*

*Literacy* has a paragraph on the scholarship boy. He says that he found working-class life suffocating. Even today, he says, he finds that thinking about it "can still induce a kind of claustrophobia." He disagrees with Hoggart that scholarship boys suffer from deracination. How many, he asks, "would choose to return to the working-class—or to any class that could properly be termed one. Scholarship boys don't require pity. On the whole this 'transplanted stock' has done well for itself, and sometimes for others too."

Enright refers rather frequently in his critical essays to Leavis, and he contributed to *Scrutiny*; but Leavis' point of view and critical methods do not seem to have influenced him very much. After leaving Cambridge, Enright taught for nearly four years at the University of Alexandria in Egypt. For the next three years he was a lecturer at Birmingham University. It was during this period, the opening years of the 1950's, that he became interested in the poets he was to anthologize in *Poets of the 1950's*. In 1953, he went, with his wife (who is French) and daughter, to Kobe, Japan, where he lectured at Konan University. During 1956–57, he taught for ten months at Free University, West Berlin. In the autumn of 1957, he went to Chulalongkorn University, Bangkok, as British Council Professor of English. Enright's journeys have not interfered very much with his being a prolific writer, nor with his awareness of developments in English literary life.

Enright has published two volumes of literary criticism, *Literature for Man's Sake* (1955) [3] and *The Apothecary Shop* (1957). [4] Actually, the two volumes contain mostly the same essays, although the former has three essays not reprinted, and the latter has several new essays. He is a frequent contributor to periodicals. Two or three of the essays, notably those on

*Coriolanus* and "Poetic Satire and Satire in Verse," are of the kind one has seen in *Scrutiny* or *Essays in Criticism:* intelligent readings of a work, with running comments on what other critics have said. But in the other essays, Enright has a line of argument that is pretty much his own.

In a piece devoted to Bonamy Dobrée's *The Broken Cistern,* Enright deplores the younger critics, those who learned their methods from Empson and Leavis. Ambiguity, Irony, Wit, and Tone—these, he says, are now more important than meaning. This is a sweeping indictment; but the remarks are illuminating insofar as they stress one of Enright's own preoccupations, a fear of a too technical criticism.

Enright also believes that critical tags inhibit original thinking and common sense. "Tradition," he says, "is such a term." Eliot's original point about the individual and the tradition was that there was a "reciprocal relation" between the two. "Today, in effect, 'tradition' is something that starts and finishes in the library: made by books, out of books, for books." What we now need, he says, is a reassertion about the importance of personality and originality.

Eliot and Auden also come in for a few criticisms. Eliot's characters in *The Waste Land* are called "pasteboard figures" and Auden's characters are called "shabby caricatures of the little man in the street." *The Cocktail Party* is seen as "living on the cinema's immoral earnings" and as almost devoid of poetry. There is the acknowledgement that *The Waste Land* helped to make the break with a faded romanticism. Enright also acknowledges a reluctant admiration for Auden, but criticizes him for his frequent presentations of abstract arguments followed by concrete images, "like an ill-fitting slipper flapping at a runner's heel."

In an article on Virginia Woolf and E. M. Forster, Enright wonders whether the stream-of-consciousness method "doesn't by its nature tend toward over-simplification instead of subtilization and dilettantism rather than a responsible seriousness." Mrs. Woolf achieves delicacy, but her lack of interest in the affairs of the public world made for an indifference to cogency. Forster, he says, has delicacy, but he has cogency too.

The doctrine that Enright has closest to heart is that we need a new humanism, and need it desperately. He ridicules the would-be pure poets who ignore ugly realities, empty rice bowls, cancer, or senility. But he deplores the Waste Land "realists." He says we must cease despising ourselves. "Unless we have found another world to live in, we had better stop our methodical 'laying waste' of this one." Public history has been dreadful in our century. But, he says, in our private histories we are "all indebted to other human beings for love and pity." These are statements he makes again and again. Modernism, he says, has been an exciting movement, but it has lived on a sense of inhumanity, desolation, and filth. If literature is to help us survive, it must present a more moderate view.

Enright's prose style is easy, supple, and humane. He has humour, although he does not have Amis' wit. He also has common sense. He is profoundly interested in what a writer is saying but probably not sufficiently interested in the way he says it.

Enright's poems have been collected in *Season Ticket* (1948),[5] *The Laughing Hyena* (1953)[6] and *Bread Rather Than Blossoms* (1956).[7] There are poems about the English Midlands, about Egypt, and Japan. Common to all but the earliest of them is an anti-art bias, as though Enright were saying that creating an artifact is less important than helping a suffering human being.

Enright's sympathies, humor and talent are best suited to writing little vignettes, such as his "University Examinations in Egypt" and "The Tourist and the Geisha." But too frequently his impulse to write poems appears to have been vitiated by his fear of pretentiousness, and his unwillingness to recognize that the poet who respects poetry as an art has sufficient reasons for creating it.

*The World of Dew* (1955) [8] is an account of post-war Japan. There are interesting chapters on education, city life, traditions, and myths. Enright believes there is an artificiality in the various traditions and ceremonies of Japan that interferes with social, economic, and political reforms. He is sufficiently realistic to observe that the over-population is such that the imagination boggles in trying to conceive any large solutions. But he suggests piecemeal reforms; and what is interfering with these, he says, is a preoccupation with the past and with traditions.

One of the minor themes running through the book is the unfortunate influence of *The Waste Land*, which is widely studied, on postwar Japan. Enright believes that the Japanese contrive to be the saddest people in the world—even though they are also capable of quiet and peaceful enjoyment. *The Waste Land* contributes to the Japanese intellectual's inclination to believe "that since the world is wholly and irrevocably waste there is nothing left to do but rake over the broken fragments in the hope of finding an exquisite bit of exquisite horribleness." Enright insists there has been far too much preoccupation with man as a feeble creature in a hopeless world. In *The World of Dew*, as in his other books, he asks for more hopefulness and more cheerfulness, both of which are in keeping with normal personal experiences.

The anthology *Poets of the 1950's* (1955) [9] was conceived as a kind of "literary missionary work."

Simply, I wanted to provide a particular audience (Japanese teachers of English literature, Japanese students, Japanese writers) with a view of what was going on (such as it was) at the moment in English poetry. A missionary element was involved—I was at the time doing all I could, in whatever way, to get the Japanese steered between the rock of Wastelanditis and the whirlpool of Dylanitis.

The introduction to *Poets of the 1950's* is devoted more to saying why the modernist movement in English poetry is at an end than to justifying or giving an account of the young poets being anthologized. He admires Eliot's technical accomplishments—he dislikes what he calls the "defeatism" of *The Waste Land.* Eliot pointed to Christianity as a way out of the waste land, but in this not everyone could join him. Auden's attitude, according to Enright, is not "compassionate anger," it is "passive cynicism." In Empson, he sees triviality expressed cleverly and ambiguously. He does admit that a few of Empson's poems provide more than mental exercises, and were a good lesson in a period when so much shapeless verse was being turned out. Even so, he does not believe Empson has been a good influence on his young imitators. Only Thomas, he says, rises above the morass of the New Apocalypse school. But Thomas's Welsh rhetoric is peculiar to him, and not to be seen as a model.

What the younger poets, those he anthologized, have in common, he says, is "chastened commonsense." They avoid obscurity because to them it seems unnecessary. He admits that some of them are a little too "academic" but the better of them, he says, should be able to find vital subjects. Enright presents few claims for their past achievements. What makes him hopeful is the new spirit to be seen in their poetry. *The Poets of the 1950's*, he says, "should be considered as an interim report—not as the presentation of a 'movement' but as the presentation of selected poems by individual writers, some of whom share common attitudes."

In Enright's two novels, *Academic Year* and *Heaven Knows Where*, we see the "new hero" abroad. His name is Packet. He grew up in a working-class family, won scholarships, and took a degree in English at Cambridge. He has no quarrel with the Welfare State. Nor does he quarrel with the fact he cannot get a university post in England. In the first novel, he is teaching in Egypt. In the second, he is a lecturer on the Island of Velo, a fictional place in the China Sea. He gets his jobs by following *The Times Educational Supplement*. It is Packet himself who "writes" the novels about his experiences.

*Academic Year* (1955) [10] is an amusing but not very skillful novel about Englishmen teaching in Egypt. The story line is too uncomplicated, and there are unnecessary scenes, in the street or in the classroom, that are a drag on its forward movement. A few of the minor characterizations are good, notably Marcel, the effeminate intellectual and dilettante, and Simone Nader, Sylvie's talkative and corpulent relative. The Egyptians, at one point, are called "a degenerate race of cheap actors," but mostly they move as part of a grey shadowy background, not as individuals. They are something like the whore, only less vivid, that Marcel, in his generosity, had provided for Packet:

> His girl had come for him. He groaned at her, he pleaded weariness, sickness, he would even have admitted to disease but felt she might not find that a cogent excuse—she merely cooed the more savagely and even laid rude hands upon him—and in the end he pushed with all the strength he could muster. There was a crash, and she disappeared from sight. What had

he done? After all, she was human, she was only earning her living. But she reappeared at the foot of the
bed, dancing and singing, a great naked blancmange.

One rather effective scene presents Packet and Sylvie, the woman he loves, on the beach. They see a dark
shape swimming toward them. It is either a dolphin,
which Packet describes as "a good and kindly animal,
and the protector of poets," or a shark. Its movement
is steady and purposeful. "It is a part of the Mediterranean seascape," Sylvie says, ironically, to him, "which
you want to join." The scene says what the novel as a
whole says. It is the sort of art that Enright is capable
of creating, but which, for reasons best known to him,
he creates too infrequently. This in another way of
saying that he does not sufficiently respect the nature
of his medium.

*Heaven Knows Where* [11] is about Packet's second
trip abroad. He has returned to England, where,
thanks to the Welfare State, he is able to have his
teeth treated free of charge. Unable to find a post in
England, he watches for notices of openings abroad.
He discovers that a lecturer in English literature is
wanted in the Island of Velo. He gets the job, and is
shortly on Velo. The King, also a Cambridge graduate,
is a tolerant, intelligent, witty man. His sister, Euphronia, has been trained in midwifery in Edinburgh. She
is a hard-headed woman. Velo itself is a not untypical
tropical island.

One of Packet's first duties is to lecture, in the Place
of Pleasure, on *The Waste Land*. Packet gives the
usual interpretations of that poem, and Euphronia
makes a hash out of Eliot's treatment of Lil, who
wanted no more children. Euphronia points out that
she had already had five, and would probably die if
she had another. Nor does she have much sympathy

with the desire of the Fisher King for more fertility. Euphronia is at one with Marie Stopes.

*Heavens Knows Where* is reminiscent of Samuel Butler's *Erewhon*, and may owe something to it. For example, the Velonians put stress on good health and cleanliness. The hospital, Euphronia's province, is clean and well equipped. But the public lavatories are magnificent. One of them looked "like a superior example of the species art gallery." The King says he "would not care to be king over a rabble of wretches who huddle behind a miserable tree or scuttle into an evil-smelling dungeon to satisfy their natural needs several times each day!" In the past, it had been the custom for families to donate a seat in memory of a dear departed one. Spitting had been so highly penalized that it had disappeared from the Island, and one of Velo's chief industries is the "manufacture of generous-sized handkerchiefs."

Despite its limitations, *Heaven Knows Where* shows that Enright has the kind of imagination that is necessary for the creation of a fictional world. *Academic Year* does not always rise above fact into fiction. *Heaven Knows Where* rises above fact into romance. But, unfortunately, Enright does not always hold the fanciful in strict enough relationship to his theme that

> Not in Utopia, subterranean fields
> Or some secreted island, Heaven knows where!
> But in the very world, which is the world
> Of all of us,—the place where in the end
> We find our happiness, or not at all!

## iv

John Holloway was born in 1920 on the Kentish edge of London. As a small boy, his family was "upper working class" but "later, speculative-builder middle class." He went to Oxford on a scholarship just before the War. After the War, he won a fellowship at All Souls College, to study philosophy. His first book was *Language and Intelligence* (1951).[12] But his interest in literature overtook his interest in philosophy and he became a lecturer in English at Aberdeen. "Going to north-east Scotland was part of giving up the teaching of philosophy and turning myself into a teacher of English." While at Aberdeen, he published *The Victorian Sage* (1953),[13] a study of the imaginative visions created by Carlyle, Disraeli, George Eliot, Newman, Arnold, and Hardy. In 1954, Holloway became English Lecturer at Cambridge University. His relationship with other Movement writers began while he was at Aberdeen.

Holloway says he was pleasantly surprised when Enright and then Conquest invited him to contribute to their anthologies. "I hadn't been writing long and hadn't published many poems." Since then, "I have met Amis a couple of times, become fairly well acquainted with Conquest, and have got to know Donald Davie well and to count him among my good friends." He has corresponded with the other contributors, but he says he thinks of himself as being "right on the edge of the group."

Holloway has written two pieces about the University Wits, one a review of some of their poetry, and the other an examination of their relationship to the Angry Young Man business. In "New Lines in English Poetry," [14] he relates their poetry to those he calls "the outsiders of the 1930's." By this phrase he means Robert Graves, Empson, and Muir. He does not spell out the specific influences, but he does say that Graves, Empson, and Muir worked within "the limitations of an exact and formal technique," and also exhibit "a radical honesty and directness." (In another place he says he himself is indebted to Muir.) He goes on to say that the University Wits, while indebted to Eliot's verse and criticism, to "close reading," to Donne—to the norms of modern poetry and criticism—are more clearly antiromantic than most of the twentieth-century poets who have preceded them. He also makes the point that these poets are for the most part from the lower classes:

> There is also another factor: less tangible, but probably vital. The poetry of the 1930's may have been left-wing, but it was profoundly upper-class. It reads "you" not "we" (Auden's "On you our interests are set your sorrows we shall not forget") like Victorian "Hymns for the Working Men." Its chief poets learnt at public (i.e. great upper-class private) schools and taught at preparatory schools. Behind it, at varying degrees of only half-discredited remoteness, stood literary Bohemia or Bloomsbury or the literary country-house weekend —the world to which, though deeply alien to it, Lawrence virtually had to gravitate because it was the literary world of his time. The recent social revolution, gentle though real, in England, has changed this. The typical "Movement" writer's childhood background appears non-conformist, often in the industrial or semi-industrial Midlands or North of England. The crucial point is, that it is on the whole staying there. If he is teaching, it is not in an upper-class preparatory school, but in a "red brick" provincial university. The automatic decanting process into upper-class England has been interrupted. Perhaps it is no longer wanted. If true, this is important: we are witnessing the end of something which has been established since the death of Keats and Hazlitt.

Holloway's own poems, collected in *The Minute* (1956),[15] are clearly Movement poems insofar as they exhibit hard-headed attitudes and a preoccupation with formal perfections. One of his primary concerns is to discover what in one poem he calls the "illustrious vernacular." In one of his reviews he says the poet's perennial task is "to achieve a unique speech that still has a massive tap-root in the inexhaustible soil of common speech." In a poem entitled "Epitaph for a Man" one finds these conversational phrases: "take notice," "merely from curiosity," "a kind of riddle," "could give him trouble," "made him uncomfortable," and others. Occasionally the insight and wit, which are invariably present in Holloway's poems, are weighed down by prosiness. But when he is writing at the top of his bent, the simplicity of the language is striking.

### v

Donald Davie says his relationship with the Movement is restricted largely to 1953–54, during which "my path intersected with that of one or two other people, notably Kingsley Amis and Philip Larkin." He says he found the experience exciting and reassuring. "However, paths that intersect begin at once to diverge and if there ever was a community of interest and aim, I think it is now dissolved, or at least it now amounts to no more than what is common to conscientious and ambitious writers in any place at any time."

He notes that whereas most of the group were from Oxford, only he and Thom Gunn were from Cambridge. But Gunn belonged to a younger generation, and he and Davie met only in 1957, in the United States.

It was an anthology, *Springtime*, 1953, which first revealed to me the existence of people who shared with me at all events an indignant distaste for the Dylan Thomas or George Barker sort of poetry which had been de rigueur in London for a decade, and which has never been eradicated there. At this period, the same people found themselves thrown into conjunction over the radio when John Wain was for a period editor of a radio magazine of new writing on the B.B.C. Third Programme. When a few reviewers and columnists noted the same connections I had seen for myself, I exerted myself bit by bit to get to know the other members of the group, all of whom I have now met except for Ennis Enright, with whom I have corresponded.

The seal, he adds, was set on the whole manifestation by the Enright and Comfort anthologies. But by the time they appeared, "I had already lost a good deal of interest."

Davie feels, however, that his social origins and his being a scholarship student give him a certain community of interest with other writers in the group:

I'm like Wain and Larkin and others in not being a product of the provinces known to the tourist, but of the industrial Midlands, in my case the South Yorkshire coalfield; and, like nearly everyone in the group I'm a product of the lower middle class, that is, of a stratum of British society in which the life of the mind is not taken for granted as taking a part of everyone's time, but rather, where it is honoured at all, has to be struggled for and is therefore embraced with more tenacity, fervour, and militancy. Accordingly, my history is the history of my education and duplicates that of all the rest—a winning of the way to one of the ancient universities by competitive examination, rather than going there as a matter of course as in the case of products of more privileged classes, such as Spender, Auden, Lehmann and Connolly and almost every writer of previous generations that you can think of.

Davie was born in 1922 in Barnsley, and attended the Barnsley Grammar School. He spent five years in the Royal Navy, eighteen months of it in North Russia and nine months in India and Ceylon. After the War he married, and returned to Cambridge for work on the Ph.D. "I differ from the rest in that the academic iron entered very deeply." From 1950 to 1957 he was Lecturer in English in Dublin University. He spent the 1957/58 academic year as a visiting professor at the University of California, Santa Barbara, and is now once again at Cambridge as a fellow. Davie is undoubtedly right in saying that the academic iron entered deeply. His two volumes of criticism are dependent upon his knowledge of eighteenth-century poetry and poetic theory.

T. S. Eliot rediscovered the seventeenth-century poets for his generation, and Davie has helped to rediscover the eighteenth-century poets for his. In the Preface to *Purity of Diction in English Poetry*,[16] he says: "I am interested in it [an eighteenth-century standard of pure diction] because I think it relevant, indeed indispensable, to the poetry of Goldsmith's generation, and to that of my own." There is also a later book, *Articulate Energy*.[17] In both, he is concerned with the diction and syntax of English poetry, particularly in the eighteenth and twentieth centuries.

"The Poet in the Imaginary Museum," [18] Davie's manifesto, is an examination of Eliot's contention that the modern poet must feel "that the whole of the literature of Europe from Homer and within it the whole of the literature of his own country has a simultaneous existence and composes a simultaneous order." Davie raises a number of questions—the relationship of a national milieu to the simultaneous order, the relationship of *one* language to the cultures from which the poet borrows, the dangers of pastiche, and so on. But the point he is really interested in, even though he develops it almost not at all, is the writing of "provincial poems," poems free from the burden of carrying within themselves a sense of the simultaneous or-

der. This is an important document for understanding
the entire group.

Davie's poems have appeared in many magazines,
in the Conquest and Enright anthologies, and in collections, *Brides of Reason*,[19] *A Winter Talent*,[20] and
*New and Selected Poems*.[21] The neo-classical influences
are everywhere evident. "The Evangelist" provides a
nice example:

> '*My brethren . . .' And a bland, elastic smile*
> *Basks on the mobile features of Dissent.*
> *No hypocrite, you understand. The style*
> *Befits a church that's based on sentiment.*
>
> *Solicitations of a swirling gown,*
> *The sudden vox humana, and the pause,*
> *The expert orchestrations of a frown*
> *Deserve, no doubt, a murmur of applause.*
>
> *The tides of feeling round me rise and sink;*
> *Bunyan, however, found a place for wit.*
> *Yes, I am more persuaded than I think;*
> *Which is, perhaps, why I disparage it.*
>
> *You round upon me, generously keen:*
> *The man, you say, is patently sincere.*
> *Because he is so eloquent, you mean?*
> *That test was never patented, my dear.*
>
> *If, when he plays upon our sympathies,*
> *I'm pleased to be fastidious, and you*
> *To be inspired, the vice in it is this:*
> *Each does us credit, and we know it too.*

In *A Winter Talent*, Davie tries to extend the range
of his poetry. He does this by loosening the metre and
employing longer lines. (Some of the poems in *A Winter Talent* appeared in the Enright and Conquest
anthologies, and for the most part these are in the

earlier manner.) Apparently Davie was disturbed by those critics of *Brides of Reason* who accused him of not daring to show his feeling. He has a poem entitled "Rejoinder to a Critic," in which he says there is a great danger in letting one's feelings loose. Even so, *A Winter Talent* is a partial letting go.

As poet, Davie is urbane, lucid, and down-to-earth. His best poems are little hymns to rationality. His critical commitments inhibit him somewhat but at the same time they have enabled him to discover and develop the convention that suits him. When imagination and feeling win victories over theory, he achieves what the eighteenth-century critics called "graces beyond the reach of art."

### vi

Someone is supposed to have said that Elizabeth Jennings' association with the Movement poets is comparable to that of a schoolmistress in a noncorridor train with a bunch of drunken marines. This may be slightly slanderous on both sides, but it says something about the tone of Miss Jennings' poetry—that it is very proper and ladylike. There is no spit, sweat, or chewing tobacco in Miss Jennings' poems, and whatever passion there is has been distilled and calmed into idea. But one should immediately add that many of the ideas are skillfully treated.

Not even the poems about landscapes or the seasons are sensuous. "A Way of Looking" says that a poem is making a landscape fit a thought. But this is not true of most of her poems. For her, it is the thought and the reflection that carry the poem, not the landscape. This is the opening of "Song at the Beginning of Autumn":

> *Now watch this autumn that arrives*
> *In smells. All looks like summer still;*

*Colours are quite unchanged, the air*
*On green and white serenely thrives.*
*Heavy the trees with growth and full*
*The fields. Flowers flourish everywhere.*

Miss Jennings generalizes about the season, and she reports her feelings.

In declining to use rhetorical gestures, startling images and metaphors, or to render the physical world with any vividness, Miss Jennings severely limits her range. She asks to be read as a poet of the mind, to be read for her insights and the play of ideas. And she selects topics about which one might write a prose essay. She likes such subjects as the nature of symbols, myth, kingship—all of which call for intellectual reach and subtlety. This is "Kings":

*You send an image out of doors*
*When you depose a king and seize his throne:*
*You exile symbols when you take by force.*

*And even if you say the power's your own,*
*That you are your own hero, your own king*
*You will not wear the meaning of the crown.*

*The power a ruler has is how men bring*
*Their thoughts to bear upon him, how their minds*
*Construct the grandeur from the simple thing.*

*And kings prevented from their proper ends*
*Make a deep lack in men's imagining;*
*Heroes are nothing without worshipping,*

*Will not diminish into lovers, friends.*

Shakespeare's Bolingbroke also knew something about the power of kingship and its accompanying symbols. When he speaks of Richard, whom he is marching to depose, he acknowledges the power he is opposing:

*Me thinks King Richard and myself should meet*
*With no less terror than the elements*
*Of fire and water, when their thundering shock*
*At meeting tears the cloudy cheeks of heaven.*
*Be he the fire, I'll be the yielding water;*
*The rage be his, whilst on earth I rain*
*My waters; on the earth, and not on him.*
*March on, and mark King Richard how he looks.*

Richard appears on the walls of the castle, and North-umberland says—

*See, see King Richard doth himself appear,*
*As doth the blushing discontented sun*
*From out the fiery portal of the east,*
*When he perceives the envious clouds are*
*To dim his glory and to stain the track*
*Of his bright passage to the occident.*

Shakespeare does not merely report on the nature of kingship and the difficulties facing those who would depose Richard—he dramatizes Richard's glory. And in the conflict of symbols one experiences the nature of the struggle. It is unfair to Miss Jennings to compare her poetry with Shakespeare's; it is not unfair to compare their methods. Vividness of language is a part of the discovery a poem makes, and Miss Jennings' insistence on the quiet manner greatly reduces the possibility of discovery.

### vii

Several of the Movement writers have said they believe that Thom Gunn may turn out to be the best poet among them. This remains to be seen. Gunn was born in Gravesend, Kent, in 1929. He attended University College School, Hampstead, and Bedales during the blitz. Before going to Trinity College, Cambridge, as a commoner, he had served for two years in the Education Corps, and spent six months in Paris.

At Trinity, he took a first in part 1 of the tripos and a good second in part 2, and he was very active with literary groups—he was president of the Cambridge English Club, he edited *Poetry from Cambridge, 1951–52*, and he wrote all of the poems that were to appear in *Fighting Terms* (1954).[22] He had also been a contributor to John Lehmann's "New Soundings" and to John Wain's "First Reading" on the B.B.C., and been anthologized in *Springtime*.

Gunn's poetry was immediately grouped with that of Wain, Davie, Larkin, and other Movement poets. In his "Poets of the Fifties," Anthony Hartley said Gunn has "a curiously unsensual passion and force of thought." He also described him as "dissenting and non-conformist, cool, scientific and analytical." Many of the poems in *Fighting Terms* are undistinguished, but a few of them have both directness and a vivid power of evocation. One of these is "A Mirror for Poets," a commentary on the Elizabethan world and its poets:

> It was a violent time. Wheels, racks and fires
> In every writer's mouth, and not mere rant.
> Certain shrewd herdsmen, between twisted wires
> Of penalty folding the realm, were thanked
> For organizing spies and secret police
> By richness in the flock, which they could fleece.
>
> Hacks in the Fleet and nobles in the Tower
> Shakespeare must keep the peace, and Jonson's thumb
> Be branded (for manslaughter), in the power
> Of irons lay the admired Southampton.
> Above all swayed the diseased and doubtful queen:
> Her state canopied by the glamour of pain.
>
> In this society the boundaries met
> Of living, danger, death, leaving no space
> Between, except where might be set

*That mathematical point whose time and place*
*Could not exist. Yet at this point they found*
*Arcadia, a fruitful permanent land.*

*The faint and stumbling crowds were dim to sight*
*Who had no time for pity or for terror:*
*Here moved the Forms, flooding like moonlight*
*In which might act or thought perceive its error.*
*The dirty details, calmed and relevant.*
*Here mankind could behold its whole extent.*

*Here in a cave the Papplagonian King*
*Crouched, waiting for his greater counterpart*
*Who one remove from likelihood may seem*
*But several nearer to the human heart.*
*In exile from dimension, change by storm*
*Here his huge magnanimity was born.*

*Yet the historians tell us, life meant less.*
*It was a violent time, and evil-smelling.*
*Jonson howled "Hell's a grammar-school to this,"*
*But found renunciation well worth telling.*
*Winnowing with his flail of comedy*
*He showed coherence in society.*

*In street, in tavern, happening would cry*
*"I am myself, but part of something great,*
*Find poets what that is, do not pass by*
*For feel my fingers in your pia mater.*
*I am a cruelly insistent friend*
*You cannot smile at me and make an end."*

Gunn says that his relationship with the Movement poets is a loose one. He has met Wain and Elizabeth Jennings while he was an undergraduate, but some of the others he met only upon his return for a visit from the United States, where he has lived since 1954. "I think the main similarity between the eight or nine of us in *New Lines*," he says, "is that we do *not* write like

the poets of the last two decades. But this similarity
becomes less when you consider that we are only writing in the tradition (if it is explicit enough to be called
a tradition) lasting from Chaucer to Hardy, that a
poem should balance the emotion with the intellect."
He also says that although he had not read Empson
or Graves until 1954 he occasionally hears or reads
that *Fighting Terms* shows clear traces of their influence. "These traces I think are probably the result of
the influences of the poets who had influenced them:
especially Donne."

After leaving Cambridge, in 1953, Gunn went to
Rome on a travelling scholarship. In 1954, he left England for a writing scholarship at Stanford. More recently he has been at the University of California,
Berkeley. He says he finds academic life congenial, and
probably will remain in the United States.

Gunn's second volume, *The Sense of Movement*,[23]
was published in 1957. Insofar as there is a unifying
theme in *The Sense of Movement* it is that the very
search for values in a valueless world is itself a value.
The poem that most fully explores this is "On the
Move." The poem describes young men obsessed with
racing motorcycles.

> *In goggles, down impersonality,*
> *In gleaming jackets trophied with the dust,*
> *They strap in doubt—by hiding it, robust—*
> *And almost hear a meaning in their noise.*

One might expect Gunn to be satiric about the young
men, but he is not. He sees them doing what all of us
are obliged to do—

> *One joins the movement in a valueless world,*
> *Choosing it, till, both hurler and the hurled,*
> *One moves as well, always toward, toward.*

And he concludes with this line—

*One is always nearer by not keeping still.*

Like some of the other Movement poets, Gunn pokes fun at arty attitudes. "Lines for a Book" teases Stephen Spender and his preoccupation with "those who were truly great." Gunn gives thanks for "all the toughs through history," for those who knew

> *That though the mind has also got a place*
> *It's not in marvelling at its mirrored face*
> *And evident sensibility.*

But Gunn is not anti-intellectual. He has poems about legends, Rome in the silver age, French novels, and paintings. But all of these interests are related to the "human condition." He admires Hemingway for the "cleanness of his writing," Stendhal for his "vigour and intelligence," and Wallace Stevens because he used "words better than anyone else in this century."

Along with two or three other Movement poets, Gunn's connection with the group is a matter both of temperament and accident. He describes his family as "middle-middle class" and more recently "upper-middle class." He describes University College School as "a minor public school." His father has been editor of a London paper, the *Daily Sketch*. The sociological question aside, Gunn's similarity to other Movement poets is fairly clear. However intense his interest in a subject or in the language used to evoke it, he sees to it that neither gets out of hand.

### viii

In the retrospect of several generations or more it is possible that none of these writers, Amis, Wain, Larkin, Miss Murdoch, or those discussed in this chapter, will loom very large; the reverse is also possible. It is most unlikely that literary historians will ignore them, because as a group they have had quite a lot to do with defining the break with the immediate past. In Samuel Johnson's lifetime, the swing away from neo-classical theory and practice had begun. In the latter years of T. S. Eliot's lifetime we have seen the swing away from Modernism.

From 1908 to World War II, the principles of Modernism dominated letters, in poetry, fiction, and in criticism. Eliot, Pound, and the Bloomsbury writers were the lawgivers. In poetry the great names, Yeats, Eliot, Stevens, and the lesser names, the Sitwells, Marianne Moore, or Cummings, were recognizably and definably modernists. The occasional poet like Robert Graves who was not a modernist was largely ignored. In fiction, the great names, Joyce, Proust, and Faulkner, were innovators, modernists. And the lesser names, Ford, Virginia Woolf, or Scott Fitzgerald, were innovators too. Twenty years ago, it was inconceivable that fiction would look to the past, back to the eighteenth century, the nineteenth century, or to the pre-modernists so castigated by Mrs. Woolf, but it has looked back.

If one or more of our writers, Kingsley Amis, or Philip Larkin, or Iris Murdoch, was clearly as gifted as Joseph Conrad, or Yeats, or Joyce, it might be easier for us to see what has happened. Traditionally the literary revolutions are a conflict between great established reputations and reputations that promise greatness. Wordsworth and Coleridge announced the end of neo-classical theory, and Pope and Johnson went into eclipse. Eliot and Pound announced that Tennyson and Swinburne suffered from imprecise emotions, and had weakened the language. An age slid under the waters of the Thames estuary.

We too have witnessed a revolution, and the New University Wits, along with many other writers, have brought it about. It has not been an especially dramatic revolution. The Welfare State, itself the greatest social revolution in England's history, has not been especially dramatic either. Perhaps it is not inappropriate that this literary revolution seems a little drab, like life in the Welfare State; it is, after all, the expression of that life.

THE NEW HERO AND A SHIFT
       IN LITERARY CONVENTIONS

"IN NOVEL AFTER NOVEL," William York Tindall says
in *Forces in Modern British Literature*, "sensitive lads
are apprenticed to life, formed by its forces, rebelling
against them, sometimes failing, sometimes emerging
in victory. . . . From 1903 onwards almost every first
novel was a novel of adolescence." Samuel Butler, he
adds, started the vogue with *The Way of All Flesh*
(1903). He wrote "this book between 1872 and 1884
to express hatred for his father, admiration for himself,
and his dearest prejudices."

Perhaps one can push the date back of 1903 to
Huysmans' *A Rebours* (1884) and his sensitive protagonist, Esseintes. From Huysmans we turn to Oscar
Wilde, to *The Picture of Dorian Gray* (1891), which
owes much to *A Rebours*. The world in which these
sensitive young men find themselves is Philistine,
money-grubbing, dull—insensitive.

Many of the novels written in this convention have
been notable contributions to modern British fiction.
There was E. M. Forster's *The Longest Journey*
(1907), Arnold Bennett's *Clayhanger* (1910), D. H.
Lawrence's *Sons and Lovers* (1913), W. Somerset
Maugham's *Of Human Bondage* (1915), and James
Joyce's *Portrait of the Artist as a Young Man* (1916).
There are many other English novels in this vein.[1]

What brought about this convention? There is probably no simple answer. In general, however, it was the sensitive artist turning away from an insensitive middle-class world, and the latter turning away from the artist. We have different names for the phenomenon, such as The Alienation of the Artist, and The Literature of Exile. The more indifferent society was to the artist the more contemptuous, the more self-consciously sensitive and sometimes the more precious the poet or fiction writer became. We will all admit that modern literature, whether in poetry, fiction, or in criticism, is *intense, alert,* self-consciously as perfect as it is possible to be. One need, in proof, only invoke the names of T. S. Eliot and Virginia Woolf. The former was so intense about the purity of poetry that he was afraid that meaning—knowing what the poet wanted to say!—would adulterate it. Mrs. Woolf would have nothing to do with middle-brow talents or tastes. Art, as she would have it, would be high-brow, or nothing.

Experimentation was characteristic of the period. Ways of telling a story were explored. There was Joyce's impersonal mode, Lawrence's characters repulsing or attracting each other as though in an emotional-electric field, and Mrs. Woolf insisting on discovering the secret life inside Mrs. Brown's head. There was the effaced narrator, the novel-of-ideas, stream-of-consciousness, and the novel seen as a poem. Yet throughout these experiments, two things usually remained constant: the protagonist, as alter ego for the novelist, continued to be the sensitive individual, and society insensitive. Usually sympathy was directed toward the protagonist, for he was among the elect, those who treasured art, literature, aesthetic states of being. There was something mysterious, almost sacred, about his sensibilities. Sometimes it was not merely society that was at fault, it was the universe itself, stonily indifferent.

*ii*

English fiction in the years since World War II has produced a new kind of protagonist. He is a rather seedy young man, and suspicious of all pretentions. He spends a lot of time in pubs, has any number of half-hearted love affairs. He gets into trouble with his landlady, his boss, and his family. There is nothing heroic about him, unless it is his refusal to be taken in by humbug. He is a comic figure, with an aura of pathos about him. *Lucky Jim* was one of the first, and is probably still the best of these novels. Keith Waterhouse's first novel, *Billy Liar* (1960) and Andrew Sinclair's *My Friend Judas* (1961) are among the most recent.

Billy Fisher is wildly imaginative. Like Jim Dixon he escapes into dream worlds; he calls them "fast excursions in Ambrosia." There he has upper-class parents who in earlier English novels were called Mater and Pater, or he carries on high-powered conversations with Bertrand Russell or Winston Churchill. Billy's own Yorkshire town is filled with "dark satanic power stations, house estates, and dark satanic teashops." Billy finds it insufferably dull.

Billy wears his sensitivity like armor. The platitudes of his father, mother and granny—who are "just folks" with a vengeance—glance off it. None of his family would recognize a subtle remark if they sat on it—and they usually do. Billy works for two funeral directors. One of them keeps a copy of *The Loved One!* not for fun, but for ideas. His co-workers are elbow prodders and tellers of soggy jokes.

Billy is a compulsive and ingenious liar, and this talent earns him, among other things he hadn't hoped to earn, three fiancées, each more horrible than the other. If one has to be *the* most horrible, it is probably Barbara. For Barbara, human emotions are something best kept wrapped in cellophane. She prefers eating oranges to making love. Once Billy puts a passion pill into a piece of candy, hoping to arouse her, but the pill makes her sleepy.

Like Jim Dixon, Billy gets into hot water with his superiors. The chief of his problems is that he has not mailed the firm's calendars, several hundred of them. Instead, he has destroyed or hidden them, and pocketed the money he had been given for postage. There are a number of ludicrous scenes concerned with getting rid of the evidence, and finally his being caught.

Billy writes comic skits, and hoped to get to London, where Success, of the sort he associates with Ambrosia, awaits him. After a number of embarrassing scenes with his mother, his fiancées, and an affair with a girl named Liz who unfortunately for Billy has wanderlust, he gets to the railroad station, headed for London. But something pulls at him, and he starts for home. Before he has gone many yards he is off on another excursion to Ambrosia.

Another recent novel is *This Sporting Life* (1960) by David Storey. Arthur Machin, the "hero," a grizzly bear type of football player, is selected to play on the company team. The followers of rugby are fierce and fanatical, and the rewards for the players, in money and prestige, are far greater than what they could expect in their grimy jobs as miners. Arthur Machin unquestioningly accepts the adulation, the social elevation, the attention of fast-living girls, and the money. On the football field his is vicious, skillful, and successful. He becomes a celebrity.

The conflict of the novel resides in the nature of the affair he has with a young widow, Mrs. Hammond, his landlady. She is as fearful and retreating as he is courageous and aggressive. Whereas the young women in Arthur's life very willingly give themselves to him, and add to the chorus of praise, Mrs. Hammond does not. She is suspicious of him, and although she accepts his gifts for herself and her two children, she does so most grudgingly. She is very ashamed in the presence of her neighbors, knowing what her reputation among them has become. Mrs. Hammond, in other words, refuses to accept the context in which Arthur Machin lives, refuses to accept his terms. Finally they separate, and she dies.

*This Sporting Life* is Arthur Machin's spiritual autobiography. He is undemonstrative and in many ways not speculative. Mrs. Hammond is also undemonstrative and unspeculative. When either arrives at a conclusion, however, there is something inevitable and final about it. Mrs. Hammond sees through pretense immediately, and there is a basic honesty to Machin's mind, even when he tries to deceive himself.

Life is hard, grim, and the towns and landscape are desolate. The brutality of the rugby matches seems an altogether fitting response to the squalor and desolation, a symbol of it. For example, "He was too slow. I was moving away when the leather shot back into my hands, and, before I could pass, a shoulder came up to my jaw. It rammed my teeth together with a force that stunned me to blackness." Machin is describing the splintering of five of his upper teeth. Despite the teeth being destroyed, he continues, after wiping his mouth off with a sponge, to play, and to play well.

The novel begins slowly. The prose seems relatively undistinguished, to have something of the grayness of the subject; and the characters are not especially interesting. But by the point, half way through the book, when the nature of the conflict becomes clear, one's attention becomes taut and never slackens. Arthur Machin, not unlike Joe Lampton, knows the taste of ashes in his mouth.

Joe Lampton, the protagonist of John Braine's widely acclaimed *Room at the Top* (1957), is a quick-witted North Country working-class boy—and he is on the make. Having experienced poverty and watched it deaden the hopes and vitality of those closest to him, he becomes fascinated by the suburban managerial class. Joe has a keen eye for economic levels—which group wears what style of suit, drives which kind of car, or uses what brand of liquors. He moves with a pure single-mindedness of purpose, determined to rise. But he has a soft spot, a flaw. He has been pursuing Susan Brown, the boss's daughter, but he falls in love with Alice, a woman ten years his senior. His opportunistic side wins, and he decides to marry Susan, who is pregnant by him. Alice, in effect, kills herself. When some-one says that no one blames him, he cries out, "Oh, my God, that's the trouble."

Alan Sillitoe's *Saturday Night and Sunday Morning*, yet another working-class novel, was published in 1959. The principal character, Arthur Seaton, is a factory hand and very similar to David Storey's Arthur Machin. He lives in a provincial city. He despises authority in any form, from the government on down. He becomes involved with the wife of a fellow worker, she becomes pregnant, and has an abortion. He begins a relationship with her sister, which is discovered by her soldier husband. The latter and a friend of his give Seaton a severe beating. While carrying on these two affairs Seaton is attracted to a young woman, whose ambition is marriage. Despite her appeal, Sea-ton resists, but finally capitulates. The plot obviously is rather commonplace and unpromising, but Sillitoe, a serious writer, presents the working-class world convincingly. His characters are wholly believable. His observed detail, even when most dreary and depressing, is often poetic.

Obviously Arthur Seaton's lustiness and conflicts with society are very close to those of Arthur Machin. The world in which he lives, and finally accepts, is the one Joe Lampton is determined to leave behind him. Neither Arthur Machin, Arthur Seaton, nor Joe Lampton belongs to the Lucky Jim type. The latter is seedy, ineffectual, comic. He is in a half-hearted contest with society, especially with the Establishment. Machin, Seaton and Lampton are in conflict with society too, but their drama is more personal and moral and heavy. Both types have the Welfare State and postwar England as a common background, but there are significant differences. The Lucky Jim type is more akin to Samuel Beckett characters such as Murphy, except that they are comic and their alienation is not so absolute.

What was behind the Lucky Jim type, what caused him? In part he is an expression of two segments of English culture in conflict, the world of "Oxford accented culture," or the gentleman's world, and the culture of a recently educated class, those who, despite their working class or lower middle-class backgrounds, have gone to Oxford or Cambridge or a provincial university.

The first of these novels, as we have seen, was Philip Larkin's *Jill* (1946), a story of wartime Oxford. *Jill* was generally ignored. John Wain created a similar hero in *Hurry on Down* (1953). Charles Lumley, fresh out of the university, takes on a succession of jobs— window cleaner, dope runner, hospital orderly, chauffeur, bouncer, writer of jokes for a radio show. Lumley is ineffectual to begin with, but his university training has compounded his inability to make a living.

The protagonist for Wain's *Living in the Present* (1955), Edgar Banks, is also the new hero: frustrated, he decides to commit a murder and then kill himself. This leads to many bizarre adventures. Finally he goes back to his job as school teacher and to the dreariness of his daily living.

Kingsley Amis' *Lucky Jim* (1954) has become the best known of the new heroes. Jim Dixon has an unerring eye for the pretentious, for the phoney, in institutions, in his colleagues (he teaches medieval history in a provincial university), and in himself. He "belongs" neither to the world of his childhood nor to the new world he inhabits, thanks to his university education and profession. He lives a strange fantasy life, and his frustrations sometimes cause him to be "quick off the mark" and sometimes a hopeless lout. But fortune favors him: he wins the girl and gets the job for which he has most talent, as a spotter of the phoney. *That Uncertain Feeling* (1955) has as hero John Lewis, a twenty-six year old satiric sub-librarian at Aberdarcy in Wales. Surrounded by drying diapers and underclothes in a small apartment, he and his family live a strictly middlebrow existence. Lewis and his wife are university graduates, but they are far from being dedicated to the pursuit of "high culture." Lewis' twin problems are controlling his lust and maintaining his integrity. Much of the book's humor is at the expense of those who are arty and pretentious. Lewis, however, is too settled to be classified with the Lucky Jim type.

Iris Murdoch's *Under the Net* (1954) has as hero Jake Donahue, a writer who makes his living as a translator. Donahue is Irish and not a product of the Welfare State, but, as an unsettled hero in an unsettled world, he has a family resemblance to Joe Lumley, Lucky Jim and Billy Fisher. And the shadowy world he inhabits, of writers, artists, theatre people

and left-wingers, is not very different from their often
dingy, dimly-lit half worlds. In her later novels she
abandons the Donahue protagonists, but her fictional
"world" remains essentially unchanged.

Dennis Enright's *Academic Year* (1954), a novel
about a young Englishman named Packet, who is
teaching in Egypt, has been called "*Lucky Jim* with
much more humanity and much less smart lacquer."
Packet also has been a "scholarship boy." Unable to
find a post in England, he takes a lectureship in Egypt.
Enright's second novel, *Heaven Knows Where* (1957)
sends Packet to the imaginary island of Velo, in the
South China Sea. The fictional world is a highly
fanciful one, but there are backward glances at the
Welfare State and at Packet's working-class origins.

One could suspect that *Happy as Larry* (1957) [2] by
Thomas Hinde was written to order. Larry Vincent, a
would-be writer, is filled with self-distrust. He is the
most loutish and ineffectual of these Lucky Jim types.
Marriage does not create in him any sense of responsibility. His wife's successful middle-class parents loom
in the background, a constant reminder of his being
a failure. He goes from one bizarre and brutal predicament to another. Everything is askew and distorted.
All he has is an unhypocritical honesty—which makes
him more pitiful than he might otherwise be. After a
series of degrading failures, he sets out to borrow
money from a friend whom he already owes several
hundred pounds and who is in the hospital because of
an accident Larry caused. One knows that the money
will not solve anything; it will merely make possible
another cycle of failure.

### iii

One of the earliest and most perceptive re-
sponses to the novel with the new hero was written
by J. B. Priestley. It is entitled "The New Novelists." [3]

Priestley decided not to mention any novelists by name—but clearly he is discussing some of the novelists listed above. He says that the *Zeitgeist* is producing the new fiction, and he minimizes the likelihood that any of the writers belong to a group. He sees them writing protest fiction—but not political protest nor protest against injustice in any form. Their novels represent a rejection of Society. At the very center of this fiction, he says, is the cry "Count us out." There is nothing militant: these novels do not openly denounce, nor do they suggest better methods of organizing society. They reject it. Priestley obviously has the Lucky Jim type in mind, not the Joe Lampton.

Priestley sees two conventions operating in these novels. One, the worlds they present seem dream-like. "These pubs, these schools and colleges, these offices, these film studios, do not seem quite solidly set in the world I know. They are rather like stage scenery out of drawing and queerly coloured." Two, their central characters are deliberately unheroic. Priestley says he finds it rather hard to sympathize with them in their misfortunes. Some of these "melancholy caddish clowns and oafs do seem to need a nurse or a probation officer rather than a chronicler and a reader." Their chief ambition is to get by. They do not plan careers or take their jobs seriously. They own only a battered typewriter or a few gramophone records. If they earn or borrow money they spend it on seedy binges. Priestley finds them the loneliest characters in all fiction. He recoils from the unheroic hero—but he adds that one must assume these novelists know what they are doing.

Priestley's main point is a good one. The image presented in these novels is that of a new form of alienation. In the nineteenth century and earlier in this century, the hero, as we have said, was often a

sensitive aesthete who pursued the arts in lonely isolation. The new hero is sometimes an oaf, sometimes an
opportunist; if he is responsible, it is usually to some
need in himself. In the little worlds of these novels,
ordinary public life and the affairs of responsible citi-
zens usually appear as though off in the distance, and
not only remote but frequently rather idiotic.

In the Christmas issue of *The Sunday Times*, 1955,
Somerset Maugham chose *Lucky Jim* as one of the
books of the year. He indicated his respect for its
author's talent, but he gave his primary attention to
the "new world" *Lucky Jim* represents and foretells:

*Lucky Jim* is a remarkable novel. It has been greatly
praised and widely read, but I have not noticed that any
of the reviewers have remarked on its ominous significance. I am told that today rather more than sixty per-
cent of the men who go to the universities go there on
a Government grant. This is a new class that has entered upon the scene. It is the white-collar proletariat.
Mr. Kingsley Amis is so talented, his observation is so
keen, that you cannot fail to be convinced that the
young men he so brilliantly describes truly represent
the class with which his novel is concerned.

They do not go to the university to acquire culture,
but to get a job, and when they have got one, scamp it.
They have no manners, and are woefully unable to deal
with any social predicament. Their idea of a celebration
is to go to a public house and drink six beers. They are
mean, malicious, and envious. They will write anonymous letters to harass a fellow undergraduate and listen
in to a telephone conversation that is no business of
theirs. Charity, kindliness, generosity, are qualities
which they hold in contempt. They are scum. They
will in due course leave the university. Some will doubt-
less sink back, perhaps with relief, into the modest class
from which they emerged; some will take to drink, some
to crime and go to prison. Others will become school-

masters and form the young, or journalists and mould public opinion. A few will go to Parliament, become Cabinet Ministers and rule the country. I look upon myself as fortunate that I shall not live to see it.

Mr. Maugham's view of the postwar generation is jaundiced and disgruntled. But he has pointed out a significant fact: the cultural life of England is passing to a new class, to those who have gone to the university on their brains and regardless of their origins. One sometimes hears that the new writers are products of the new red-brick universities—but Mr. Maugham is generally right in saying "the university," by which he means Oxford or Cambridge. Mr. Maugham singles out their beer drinking for censure—but this is probably only a symptom of their representing a newer, perhaps still inchoate, culture, one that is different from Maugham's traditional "gentleman culture."

A couple of weeks later (January 8, 1956), C. P. Snow replied to Mr. Maugham. His letter does not censure the generation described by Amis—it attempts to account for their actions and feelings.

Sir,—

I was distressed by Mr. Maugham's remarks about Mr. Kingsley Amis's *Lucky Jim*. We have taken it for granted for so long that anything Mr. Maugham writes will be generous, temperate, and sensible. We shall of course go on thinking of him so; but this outburst was none of those things.

Why is it so contemptible to go to a university on a Government grant? Why is it so bestial to celebrate by drinking pints of beer? Mr. Amis has invented a highly personal comic style, and this style seems to have gone to the heads of some readers, Mr. Maugham surprisingly among them. At least I can see no other explanation why a wise man should regard Mr. Amis's favourite characters as horrors. It would be more justifiable to see them as the present-day guardians of the puritan conscience—enraged by humbug, unrealistically shocked by the compromises and jobberies of the ordinary worldly life, more anxious than their seniors to show responsibility to those whom they love or who love them.

They seem to me very much like the bright young men who came, as I did myself, from the same social origins twenty-five or thirty years ago. I can see only one significant difference. In my time bright young men from the lower middle classes did not regard themselves as socially fixed; they thought there was a finite chance that they might some day live as successful men had lived before them.

Mr. Amis's characters cannot and do not imagine this for themselves. Starting with no capital, Lucky Jim will not accumulate enough money to change his way of life. He is never going to starve, but he cannot have a dramatic rise in the world, and he will not be able to leave money to his children.

It is an unexpected result of the Welfare State that in this sense it should make the social pattern not less rigid but much more so. Mr. Amis's characters take it with a grin, but, like all people clamped down in a rigid society, they sometimes feel that the whole affair is no concern of theirs.

V. S. Pritchett is another of the older writers who has tried to characterize and evaluate these novelists. His article is entitled "These Writers Couldn't Care Less." [4] His is not a sympathetic account, but it is not so unsympathetic as its title implies. The hostile side of his argument is his claim that the central characters in these novels are trimmers and pursuers only of self-interest. On the other hand, he sees their authors as a new class of uprooted people, belonging neither to the class of their origins nor committed to the "dying culture" of the "class for which they can now qualify."

Pritchett also makes some useful remarks about the style and structure of many—certainly not all—of these novels. It tends to be, he says a "talking style of people making war upon the assumptions of the middle-class culture, by refusing to wear its masks. It is a debunking style." Certainly it is true that much of the writing has the quality of a rather vulgar voice, using hit-or-miss expressions. When the occasion is right, it is effective because it is satirizing the tones of the "educated voice" and objects venerated by those who take pride in their cultivation.

Secondly, Pritchett points out that a number of these novels are picaresque. These young novelists "discerned that the picaresque novelists were products of revolution: that they were engaged in adventure; and the modern adventure was a rambling journey from one conception of society to another."

Varied formulas have been given to account for the new hero. Geoffrey Gorer, in "The Perils of Hypergamy," says his tensions are consequent upon marrying into a higher class than that of his origins. This accounts in part for Joe Lampton, and Larry Vincent. Jim Dixon marries out of his class too, but by the time he does so, his tensions seem to be behind him. Hypergamy is not a problem for most of the other new heroes. Perhaps one should say that the new hero has problems that grow out of his essential classlessness.

The moods of a generation or a nation are not easy to diagnose—and the mood of the postwar writer in the British Welfare State is no exception. Probably there is no single mood. But common to most of these novels is an air of being hemmed-in, restricted, of characters trying to find their way in new social and cultural situations.

*iv*

Clearly shifts in literary conventions are in response to social changes. English fiction, in the past, was mostly a product of upper-class culture. Settings could include middle- and upper-class homes, country houses, and expensive flats, nannies, tutors, public schools, and long weekends. This more recent fiction is likely to describe institutions, small libraries, hospitals, or village governing offices. It can exhibit small flats, slick picture magazines, radio programs, jazz records, movies, and pubs. It is a world largely Americanized.

The very style and structure of the novels are appropriate to the world the fiction evokes. The style has none of Virginia Woolf's literary elegance, and carefully thought-out metaphors, E. M. Forster's urbanity, or Joyce's preciseness. This latter style is less concerned to awe, or to create a lasting, impersonal work of art. It is likely to be flip, as though out of the side of the author's mouth, to be closer to bright journalism.

Virginia Woolf criticized the conventions of Arnold Bennett, H. G. Wells, and John Galsworthy. In general, she objected to the *externality* of life in their novels. "Life," she said in a now famous sentence, "is not a series of gig lamps symmetrically arranged; but a luminous halo, a semi-transparent envelope surrounding us from the beginning of consciousness to the end." For her generation, for the moderns, or for the "Georgians" as she also called them, "the point of interest lies very likely in the dark places of psychology."

The authors of the postwar fiction discussed above have ceased being interested in the murky darkness of the individual consciousness, the light and shadow in an isolated mind. The characters are social beings insofar as they play roles in society, as students, employees, or young men jimmying a lock and trying not to be caught. Emphasis is on the action, the movement of the story. There is neither interest in nor time for explorations of a single consciousness, such as Mrs. Woolf explored in Clarissa Dalloway or Mrs. Ramsay. The author's point of focus is external, and his tone, appropriately, likely to be satiric.

We have been discussing two types of "heroes" in British fiction since World War II. Obviously there are many novels excluded from consideration. For example, Lawrence Durrell's Alexandrian quartet, recently and justifiably acclaimed, does not belong in either of our categories. His four novels are a successful experiment in technique, a continuation of experiments that go back to Proust, Joyce and Faulkner. The technique has sometimes been called the principle of "simultaneity"; Joseph Frank called it the "doctrine of spatial form." William Golding's *Lord of the Flies* and other books, also justifiably acclaimed, suggests a kinship with the novels of the years of the great experiments. It suggests the anti-utopian novels of Aldous Huxley and George Orwell.

Another group is represented by such names as Joyce Cary, Anthony Powell, L. P. Hartley, C. P. Snow, and Angus Wilson. Despite their mid-century preoccupations their novels seem related to the solidities of an older world, say the Edwardians, in some ways akin to Galsworthy, but not to John Braine or Kingsley Amis. Even so, one detects a similarity of another sort: all of them, Cary, Snow, Amis or Miss Murdoch appear largely indifferent to the experiments of the twenties and thirties.

To return to our creators of two types of "heroes" in post World War II fiction: There is little to be gained at this point in claiming that Amis is among the finest comic talents since Wells or Evelyn Waugh, or that Miss Murdoch is a philosophical novelist of such and such an order, or that John Braine is as subtly preoccupied with money and caste as Arnold Bennett was. They should not be asked to carry the burden of such criticism until they are more firmly established and have many more novels to their credit.

What is clear is that these writers have produced a different set of literary conventions. The books of John Braine and David Storey are not very different from Bennett's, and deal with their subjects in a manner he might have employed. They leap back of Mrs. Woolf and Joyce—to the pre-modern Bennett. And as we have seen some of their older contemporaries have done the same thing. The Lucky Jim type, which originated and developed in The New University Wits group, is new. He and his kind have appeared with enough frequency and are of sufficient interest to have won a small place for themselves in the history of English letters.

LITERARY CONVENTIONS DEVELOP, thrive, and eventually wear themselves out. They develop because a poet, fiction writer, or dramatist finds a new way of looking that is strikingly appropriate and meaningful. After World War I, to take an example, young writers felt not merely that they had been betrayed but that true idealism was impossible in a money-minded materialistic world. Eliot wrote *The Waste Land*, and it became the central image for a generation of writers. Hart Crane in *The Bridge* attempted to answer it, but managed for the most part only to reaffirm its central thesis. Fitzgerald and Faulkner did American versions of it in *The Great Gatsby*, *The Sound and the Fury*, and *Pylon*. Poets and fiction writers borrowed a point of view from it, as well as themes and phrases; Robert Sherwood, for example, used it as the central image in *The Petrified Forest*.

In the 1930's Auden and others improvised on it, using machinery rusted and unused in the fields, abandoned mines, long weekends in which members of the upper classes talked like characters in Eliot's poem. Anticipating war, Auden also used such images as trains carrying soldiers into the very suburbs of The Waste Land, and passports being cancelled.

An image closely related to the waste land was

established by Hemingway in *The Sun Also Rises* and
A *Farewell to Arms*: a world always at war. Eliot's
poem had an idiom seemingly appropriate to his
subject, and Hemingway had an idiom appropriate to
his. Young men went into World War II carrying
these images in their heads, of the world as a waste
land and a world ceaselessly at war. Eliot's vision lived
in the imaginations of sophisticates and intellectuals.
Hemingway's vision had a more universal appeal, and
Hemingway was a culture hero for aspiring novelists
and for soldiers everywhere. Some of the poems written during the War sounded the Eliotic note, and
far too many of the novels reproduced, in an uncon-
vincing way, the Hemingway hero and the taut sentence.

Gradually, since the Second War, these images
have tended to fade. Is the world truly a waste land?
Is this what we believe in our daily lives? Is our age
more of a waste land than was the age of Julius Caesar
or the age of Bismarck? Again, do we live in a world
constantly at war, or in an age desperately trying to
achieve peace? Eliot's vision and Hemingway's vision
no longer have the relevance they had for the 1920's,
1930's and the war years. Because they do not have it,
poets and fiction writers are likely to discover newer,
more appropirate images. In the process they are
likely to abuse their eminent elders, much in the way
Eliot and Pound abused Tennyson and Swinburne,
and Hemingway abused the writers in the Genteel
Tradition and, more immediately, Sherwood Anderson.

In the years between the two wars Art, for many,
was a kind of religion. If one could not lend his
sympathies very wholeheartedly to social or political
causes, he might live in the tower of art. Perhaps it
is not wholly accidental that the tower looms so

dramatically in Joyce and Yeats—it is a symbol of their dedication to art and their isolation from society. There were patron saints of art—"His true Penelope was Flaubert." Eliot listed those authors who belonged to the true tradition and he chastised those he found to be uncanonical. Auden wrote poems about James and Melville and the other saints of letters. Certain writers, like Lawrence, felt that they themselves were the true prophets. It is not an exaggeration to say that a great air of reverence and hushed expectancy hung over literary discussions, as though in anticipation of a kind of Second Coming. Precisely in what form this event would occur one could not be sure—but by attending closely to the Altar of Art one would be ready.

All this seems to have gone. Eliot's quest for the grail and for the still moment in the rose garden belongs to an earlier era. His later plays are almost embarrassingly ordinary and sentimental. Auden, in middle age, writes with a limpness that the youthful Auden would have parodied mercilessly. And the memory of Spender's having thought continuously about those truly great seems naïvely youthful and romantic. Poor Dylan Thomas, drunk with rhetoric, could suffer tedium only briefly and drank himself to death.

In fiction, the hero is no longer a hero—he doesn't even reverence art. And the creators of the new hero take a rather dim view of culture heroes, whether it be Flaubert, James, or the Common Man. Figures to whom they refer rather favorably on occasion, such as George Orwell, Robert Graves, and F. R. Leavis, are curiously unsatisfactory heroes. Orwell, excellent as he was at uncovering sham, seems to have worn a continual sneer. Graves is a moderately successful poet and fiction writer, an honest critic, but a man whose cantankerousness reaches outlandish and unintentionally funny proportions. Leavis' fervor and

moral intensity can be quite moving, but his in-
tolerance of aimless vitality is frightening; one feels
he would willingly blow Falstaff and Uncle Toby off
the face of the earth and feel he had done his stint
that day for righteousness and moral improvement.
The postwar generation appears not to like their
heroes pure, and to want built-in protections against
any form of inflation, whether in political leaders,
culture heroes, fictional characters, or language itself.
They have, for example, reacted strongly against the
modernist style in poetry.

Eliot, Pound and many of their imitators contributed to a period style. A highly personal and
idiosyncratic manner, and obscurity are part of the
modernist idiom. Pope and Swift wrote with an "aggressive clarity." To do so was an ideal of neo-classical
writing. The obscurity of Eliot, Pound, the Sitwells,
Stevens, Crane, and others was also "aggressive."

Randall Jarrell once characterized the idiom of
modernist poetry in these terms:

> very interesting language, a great emphasis on connota-
> tion, texture; extreme intensity, forced emotion—vio-
> lence; a good deal of obscurity; emphasis on sensation,
> perceptual nuances; emphasis on details, on the part
> rather than on the whole; experimental or novel quali-
> ties of some sort; a tendency toward external formless-
> ness and internal disorganization—these are justified,
> generally, as the disorganization required to express a
> disorganized age, or alternatively, as newly-discovered
> and more complex types of organization; and extremely
> personal style—*refine your singularities*; lack of re-
> straint—all tendencies are forced to their limits; there
> is a good deal of emphasis on the unconscious, dream-
> structure, the thoroughly subjective.

He wrote this in 1940, and if one examines the poems
in the last issues of *The Southern Review*, in *Kenyon*,
*Sewanee*, and *Poetry* or British journals at that time

it is clear that Jarrell is describing a period style. Important poets individualize a period style. The lesser ones, and those who achieve only pastiche, in the retrospect of a generation eventually seem dated. Jarrell's account is of a poetic idiom that no one any longer aspires to write.

In 1961, the third Methuen Anthology of Modern Verse, 1940–1960, was issued. Its editor is Elizabeth Jennings. The poems represented in it begin with the period of Eliot's *Four Quartets* and cover five years of the last war and more than ten years of the Cold War. Miss Jennings says the major themes in the poetry of the last twenty years are suffering, restlessness and uncertainty. She adds that the feelings of disorder might have led to a fragmented, disorderly style, but this, she finds, is not the case. "On the contrary, with the exception of a short-lived movement called the Apocalyptics which appeared during the forties, the most marked characteristic of the period . . . is a sense of order, an urge to clarity, a leaning toward formal perfection." It almost seems, she says, that poets have taken their cue from William Empson, and have learned "a style from despair." Poetry, she adds, is making a plea for order in a universe of confusion and chaos.

As one might expect, Miss Jennings finds Philip Larkin, Thom Gunn, Donald Davie, John Wain and Enright to be among the most interesting poets who emerged after the war. What one might not expect, however, is the appearance of so many poets who share a passion for metrical propriety, lucidity, and order.

Certain older poets, senior to the University Wits by seven, ten or twelve or even twenty-odd years, have attained a greater eminence. Two decades ago few would have admired their tidiness. Thomas Blackburn, Norman MacCaig, Anne Ridler, William Empson, and especially Robert Graves emerge with a new sense of belonging, with a new air of importance. Their talents are not esentially different from what they were a generation ago. It is that a new period style is developing that better suits their individual gifts or talents.

Eliot once said that a poet writing in the twentieth century and experiencing its complexities had no choice but to be obscure. No critic would be likely to say that nowadays. It would seem, what it probably was, an effort to rationalize the modernist idiom. In fiction, too, the modernist idiom has been under attack, at least by implication. The Jamesian sentence, well hung, weighted with parentheses, intensely concerned with nuance and shading, would be ironically inappropriate in novels that stress quick movement, economic strains, and getting on with the job at hand. Virginia Woolf's metaphors and elegantly phrased observations are appropriate to characters deeply concerned with their own feelings and looking into their own consciousness. They would be inappropriate in novels taking off a Jim Dixon when drunk or getting into a fight with someone trying to take his girl away from him. Every sentence James Joyce wrote was resonant with the history of Western literature. None of the younger writers, with the possible exception of Iris Murdoch, indicates any real awareness of tradition. The age of experiment appears to be over. A new style has emerged. In poetry, it is earthy, analytical, and "aggressively" honest. In fiction it aspires to be a non-style. It is a style nonetheless, because it is trying to get beneath sham and pretentiousness.

Graham Hough in his recent book, *Reflections on a Literary Revolution*, on the poetics of Eliot and Pound and related matters, makes a pertinent point:

Two influential novelists of the present generation who are not at all parochial but very much men of the world, Mr. Angus Wilson and Sir Charles Snow, have expressed or implied or suggested a large lack of interest in the experimental fiction of the twenties; their suasions are toward the large-scale socially oriented novel, the presentation of the world as it actually works, without any fiddle-faddle about form and verbal nicety.

Mr. Hough enters a demurrer or two on the dangers of slipping too far away from concern with form and verbal niceties. But the point remains. He ties the modernist movement in poetry to the modernist movement in fiction:

> But we can now discern a much larger and more general reason for the restricted influence of the new poetry. It was not the vehicle of great spiritual force; it did not have behind it the flow and impetus of a great movement of society and ideas.

The first waves of the Romantic Movement, he says, had behind them the flow and impetus of such a current and ideas. By implication he is saying that an isolated or "exiled" literature, however brilliant its techniques, will not serve as a powerful leavening moral force; it will merely exhibit the sensibilities of its authors.

If Hough is right, post World War II novelists, the question of their respective talents aside, have returned the novel to its traditional role, the relation of man to man in society. Probably the preoccupations of the experimenters of the twenties and thirties will not be ignored. They can be used in newer ways but not as ends in themselves.

The excitement and enthusiasm caused by a literary movement might lead one into feeling that preceding literary movements and generations were a preparation for the ultimate and final movement, the present one. This of course would be a delusion. In a given literary generation there may be many exceedingly gifted writers, and some men of genius, and collectively they create a style. The style gives a sense of order to the hopes and urgencies of the time, and at its best may speak most reassuringly, and at a level beneath which no further questions can be formulated. Then the age begins to shift and alter, and new questions are formulated. A younger group of writers becomes dissatisfied with the style, and begins to create another. This is what we have seen happen in England since World War II. The modernist movement is now seen as belonging essentially to the era between the wars. Its poetry and fiction already begin to look a little strange and foreign, seemingly to belong to an earlier era, as indeed they do.

### 1—A New Literary Generation

1. August 27, 1954, pp. 260–1.
2. October 1, 1954.
3. *Twentieth Century*, December, 1956, pp. 499–505.
4. Kenkyusha, Tokyo, 1955.
5. Macmillan and Company, Ltd., 1956.

### 2—Philip Larkin

1. Fortune Press.
2. Fortune Press.
3. Faber and Faber, 1947. Reissued in 1956.
4. The Marvell Press, Hessle, East Yorkshire. Published here by St. Martin's Press.
5. Fantasy Press, Oxford University Press.

### 3—John Wain

1. October 26, 1957, p. 285.
2. Reading University School of Art.
3. Routledge and Kegan Paul, Ltd.
4. Harrap, Ltd., 1953.
5. Routledge & Kegan Paul, Ltd.
6. Macmillan, London.
7. "Orwell in Perspective," *New World Writing*, No. 12.
8. *Sewanee Review*, Summer, 1957, LXV, 3, pp. 353–74.
9. March 16, 1958, p. 17.

10. Secker and Warburg. *Hurry On Down* was reprinted in 1955.

11. Secker and Warburg.

12. Macmillan and Company, Ltd.

13. Macmillan, London.

### 4—Iris Murdoch

1. Miss Murdoch wrote a distinguished essay entitled "Metaphysics and Ethics" for *The Nature of Metaphysics* (London: Macmillan, 1957).

2. Miss Murdoch's six novels have been published in London by Chatto and Windus, in the United States by the Viking Press. The pagination of quoted material is of the American edition.

3. *The Listener*, March 16, 1950, pp. 473, 476.

4. *The Listener*, March 23, 1950, pp. 523–4.

5. (New Haven, Conn.: Yale University Press, 1953), 78 pages.

6. *The Yale Review*, XLIX, No. 2 (Winter, 1960), 247–281.

7. See also "The Sublime and The Good," *Chicago Review*, XIII, No. 3, (Fall, 1955), 42–55.

8. *The Unofficial Rose* (Viking, 1962) is not unlike her earlier novels in that it is mannered and tautly intellectual, but it is also more compassionate. Miss Murdoch's preoccupation with philosophy is also less evident in this novel.

### 5—Kingsley Amis

1. Amis has written an account of his school days in "City Ways," *The Spectator*, February 28, 1958.

2. *Twentieth Century*, August, 1956.

3. *Spectator*, December 31, 1954.

4. *Spectator*, April 1, 1955.

5. *Spectator*, February 3, 1956.

6. *Spectator*, August 12, 1955.

7. *New York Times Book Review*, July 7, 1957.

8. School of Art, Reading University.

9. Fantasy Press, Oxford. Victor Gollancz have pub-

lished Amis' novels; Ballantine Books published his *New Maps of Hell* (1960) on science fiction, and Harcourt, Brace and World issued *Spectrum: A Science Fiction Anthology* (1962) which he edited with Robert Conquest.

10. Amis' own account of Jim Dixon does not mention the legendary or archetypal nature of his hero: "Dixon is supposed to be the son of a clerk, an office worker (like myself). He is a Labour Party socialist and probably took part in student politics when younger (like myself). One is meant to feel that he did well enough in his student academic career to make it natural for him to become a history lecturer, which he did without much thought. Though he finds the academic world decreasingly to his taste, he sticks at it because he does think university teaching an important job, and also because he is afraid of venturing out on his own. I think he is a plausible figure in his world: there are certainly many like him in that they are the first generation in their families to have received a university education, they have won their way up by scholarships all through, they are not the conventional Oxford-Cambridge academic type (sherry, learned discussion, tea-parties with the Principal's wife, chamber concerts) but stick to their own, to the ones their non-academic contemporaries share (beer, arguments in pubs, amorous behavior at—and outside—dances, jazz). Dixon has seen, throughout his life, power and position going to people who (he suspects) are less notable for their ability than their smooth manners, their accents, the influence they or their fathers can wield. The money thing is less important; Dixon is hard-up himself, and is a bit suspicious of the rich, but is far more so of Oxford-accented "culture." If he were closely questioned about this, he would probably admit in the end that culture is real and important and ought not to be made the property of a sort of exclusive club which you can only enter if you come from the right school—culture ought to be available to everyone who can use it; but such an avowal would be very untypical of him and you would probably have to get him very drunk first."

11. Edited by Tom Maschler, MacGibbon and Kee, 1957.

### 6—The Other Writers

1. Macmillan and Co., Ltd., 1955.
2. Ward, Lock and Co., Ltd., London.
3. Kenkyusha, Ltd., Tokyo.
4. Secker and Warburg.
5. Aux Editions du Scarabee, Alexandria, Egypt.
6. Routledge & Kegan Paul, Ltd., London.
7. Secker and Warburg, London.
8. Secker and Warburg, London.
9. Kenkyusha.
10. Secker and Warburg.
11. Secker and Warburg, 1957. Enright has also published a "thriller," *Insufficient Poppy* (1960), and another book of poems, *Some Men Are Brothers* (1960). Both were published by Chatto and Windus. In 1957 he co-edited *Poetry of Living Japan*, Grove Press.
12. Macmillan & Co. Ltd.
13. Macmillan & Co. Ltd.
14. *The Hudson Review*, IX, Winter, 1955–57.
15. The Marvell Press.
16. Chatto and Windus, 1952.
17. Routledge and Kegan Paul, 1955.
18. *The Listener*, July 11 & 18, 1957.
19. Fantasy Press, Oxford, 1955.
20. Routledge and Kegan Paul, London, 1957.
21. Wesleyan University Press, 1961.
22. Fantasy Press, Oxford.
23. Faber and Faber. Gunn's most recent volume is *My Sad Captain* (University of Chicago Press, 1961).

### 7—The New Hero and a Shift in Literary Conventions

1. In America, the sensitive protagonist in an insensitive world was to be seen in Scott Fitzgerald's Amory Blaine (*This Side of Paradise*, 1920), John Dos Passos' John Andrews (*Three Soldiers*, 1921), Ernest Heming-

way's Nick Adams (*In Our Time*, 1924), William Faulkner's Bayard Sartoris (*Sartoris*, 1929), and Thomas Wolfe's Eugene Gant (*Look Homeward, Angel*, 1929). There are, of course, many similar novels in twentieth-century American fiction. We almost assume, in picking up a novel, that the protagonist will be poetic in temperament and in conflict with an indifferent, materialistic society.

2. *Billy Liar* was published by W. W. Norton in the United States, *My Friend Judas* by Simon and Schuster, *This Sporting Life* by Macmillan, and *Saturday Night and Sunday Morning* by Knopf. *Room at the Top* was published in England by Eyre and Spottiswood and *Happy as Larry* by MacGibbon and Kee.

3. *The New Statesman and Nation*, June 26, 1954.

4. *The New York Times Book Review*, April 28, 1957.

# INDEX

À Rebours, 133
Academic Year, 115–17
"Aiming at a Million," 83
Allen, Walter, 5
"Along the Tightrope," 43
Amis, Kingsley, 1, 10, 14, 33, 75–102, 120
Angry Young Man, 1
The Apothecary Shop, 110–11
Auden, Wystan Hugh, 85, 150

Bayley, John, 55
B.B.C., 32, 127
Beckett, Samuel, 54
The Bell, 65–66
Bennett, Arnold, 33, 39–40, 133
Billy Liar, 135–36
Blackburn, Thomas, 154–55
Bloomsbury, 13, 15
"Born Yesterday (for Sally Amis)," 26
Bradbury, Malcolm, 6
Bread Rather Than Blossoms, 112
Brides of Reason, 123
Butler, Samuel, 133
Byron, Lord, 79

A Case of Samples, 82
Conquest, Robert, 1, 7, 10, 11, 77, 103–9, 118

Contemporary Reviews of Romantic Poetry, 37
The Contenders, 48–50, 52, 53

Davie, Donald, 6, 7, 10, 77, 103, 120–24, 154
Declaration, 43–44

Eliot, T. S., 122, 134, 151–52, 154, 155
Empson, Wm., 11, 34, 118, 155
"English Poetry: The Immediate Situation," 41–42
Enright, Dennis, 1, 9, 10, 85, 103, 109–17, 118, 154
"The Evangelist," 123
Existentialism, 66–68
"The Existentialist Hero," 67–68

Fighting Terms, 127–29
The Flight from the Enchanter, 59–62, 70
Forster, E. M., 112, 133
Fraser, G. S., 6, 29, 35

"Gentleman aged five before the Mirror," 35–36
A Girl in Winter, 20–23
Going, 2
Graves, Robert, 34, 118, 131, 155

Gunn, Thom, 6, 7, 77, 103, 120, 126–30, 154

Hamilton, I., 6
*Heaven Knows Where*, 109, 116, 117
Hemingway, Ernest, 151
Hoggart, Richard, 109–10
Holloway, John, 10, 77, 103, 117–20
Hongh, Graham, 155–56
*Hurry on Down*, 44–46

*I Like It Here*, 94–96
*In Our Time*, 163
*Interpretations*, 37–38

Jarrell, Randall, 153
Jennings, Elizabeth, 10, 103, 124–26, 154–55
*Jill*, 17–20
Joyce, James, 151–52

"Kings," 125–26

"The Landing in Deucalion," 106–7
*Language and Intelligence*, 118
Larkin, Philip, 5, 7, 10, 14, 16–29, 76–77, 120, 121, 155
*The Laughing Hyena*, 112
"Laughter To Be Taken Seriously," 81
Lawrence, D. H., 78, 80
Leavis, F. R., 5, 109
Lehmann, John, 8–9, 127
*The Less Deceived*, 16, 17, 28
Literary Conventions, 147–56
"The Literary Critic in the University," 38–39
*Literature for Man's Sake*, 110
*Living in the Present*, 46–48

*The Longest Journey*, 133
*Look Homeward, Angel*, 163
*Lucky Jim*, 135, 139, 140
Lucky Jim. *See also* "The Unheroic Hero"

MacCaig, Norman, 155
*Maps of Hell*, 161
Maugham, Somerset, 143–44
*Maverick*, 12–13
"Metaphysics and Ethics," 160
*The Minute*, 119–20
"A Mirror for Poets," 127–28
*Mixed Feelings*, 34
Modernism, 131–32, 134–35
"Movement," 1–15
*Murdoch*, Iris, 1, 55–74, 81
*Murphy*, 54
*My Friend Judas*, 135

*New and Selected Poems*, 123
The New Hero. *See* "The Unheroic Hero"
*New Lines*, 11–12, 105, 128–29
*New Maps of Hell*, 78
*New Poems, A P.E.N. Anthology*, 104
New University Wits, 1–15
*Next, Please*, 25–26
*The North Ship*, 17
"A Note on Wyatt," 84
*Nuncle*, 52–53

"Ode to the West Wind," 62
*Of Human Bondage*, 133
Orwell, George, 5, 40–41, 78

*Pasternak Affair*, 104
Peacock, Thomas Love, 79–80
P.E.N., 12

*The Picture of Dorian Gray*, 133

*Poems*, 82

"The Poet in the Imaginary Museum," 122–23

"Poetry of Departures," 28

*Poets of the 1950's*, 1, 110, 113–15

*Portrait of the Artist as a Young Man*, 133

Pound, Ezra, 153, 155

*Preliminary Essays*, 31, 38–42

Priestley, J. B., 141–43

Pritchett, V. S., 145–46

*Purity of Diction in English Poetry*, 122–23

Queneau, Philip, 54–55

Read, Sir Herbert, 16

"Reasons for Attendance," 27

*Reflections on a Literary Revolution*, 155–56

"Restoration Comedy and its Modern Critics," 39

Ridler, Anne, 35, 155

Romantic Movement, 155–56

St. John's College, Oxford, 10

*The Sandcastle*, 62–64, 70

*Sartoris*, 163

*Sartre, Romantic Rationalist*, 67–68

*Saturday Night and Sunday Morning*, 138–39

Scott, J. D., 6

*Scrutiny*, 110

*Season Ticket*, 112

*A Severed Head*, 70–74

Sillitoe, Alan, 138–39

Sinclair, Andrew, 135

Snow, Sir Charles, 144–45

*Socialism and the Intellectuals*, 98–100

"Song at the Beginning of Autumn," 124–25

*Spectator*, 5–7, 9, 78–79, 108

Spender, Stephen, 4–5, 6, 130

*This Sporting Life*, 136–37

*Springtime*, 121

Storey, David, 136–37

"The Sublime and Beautiful Revisited," 68–69

Swansea, 77

*Take a Girl Like You*, 96–98

*That Uncertain Feeling*, 90–94

Third Programme, 8–9

*This Side of Paradise*, 162

Thomas, Dylan, 80

*Three Soldiers*, 162

Tindall, Wm. York, 133

Tradition, 111–12, 122–23

*A Travelling Woman*, 50–52, 53

*Under the Net*, 54–59, 70

The Unheroic Hero: Jake Donahue, 140, 141; Jim Dixon, 75, 77, 85–90, 139, 140, 155; Charles Lumley, 43, 139; Packet, 115–17, 141; Larry Vincent, 141

*The Uses of Literacy*, 109–10

*The Victorian Sage*, 118

Wain, John, 1, 5, 6, 11, 14, 30–53, 81, 120, 121, 154

*The Waste Land*, 111–12, 113, 150–51

Waterhouse, Keith, 135–36

*The Way of All Flesh*, 133

The Welfare State, 131–32

"When It Comes," 36–37

Wilde, Oscar, 133

Wilson, Colin, 3
A Winter Talent, 123
Woolf, Virginia, 112, 131, 133, 134, 154–55
A Word Carved on a Sill, 34
The World of Dew, 113

A World of Difference, 108–9
Wuthering Heights, 42
Wyatt, Woodrow, 1

Yeats, Wm. Butler, 17